Hospice Voices:

A Message

by

Ellen M. Mitchell

PublishAmerica
Baltimore

© 2010 by Ellen M. Mitchell.
All rights reserved. No part of this book may be reproduced, stored in a retrieval system or transmitted in any form or by any means without the prior written permission of the publishers, except by a reviewer who may quote brief passages in a review to be printed in a newspaper, magazine or journal.

First printing

PublishAmerica has allowed this work to remain exactly as the author intended, verbatim, without editorial input.

ISBN: 978-1-4489-9320-8 (softcover)
ISBN: 978-1-4489-7744-4 (hardcover)
PUBLISHED BY PUBLISHAMERICA, LLLP
www.publishamerica.com
Baltimore

Printed in the United States of America

Dear Jan —
God will
always be with
you! Feel His arms
around you! God bless!
Ellen

Acknowledgments

I would like to thank Allan and Rosemary Young who helped me to arrange this book. I could not have finished it without their support and encouragement. Thank you to Don Piper who I heard speak about his books, *90 Minutes in Heaven* and *Heaven Is Real*. He helped me realize that after retirement and health issues I had a new normal. I can't wait to see what God has in store for me now. A big hug and thank you to my husband Jay, who, also never stopped encouraging me. To my friends, thank you for nudging me when I needed it the most. Thank you to all of my patients and families. What an inspiration you were. Thank you for gently pushing me to write down the experiences God gave to all of us. To my grandchildren I give many, many hugs. Your part in the story gave me the idea to write many years ago. Most of all, thank you God for the courage to write and to finish. It is Your message.

INDEX

THE BEGINNING 9
MY FATHER'S DEATH—MY FIRST 12
PASS IT ON! 15
TWO ANGELS 17
MY MOTHER IN HEAVEN 19
MY MOTHER'S DEATH 21
EIGHT O'CLOCK 24
"I WANT TO GO HOME" 26
CAN I BRING HER WITH ME? 28
A LOVE STORY 30
A COUNTRY GRAVESIDE SERVICE 33
"TELL THEM TO SING" 35
THE ANGEL MAN 37
LADY, I BELIEVE YOU 43
A SENSE OF HUMOR 44
"PLEASE TELL THEM I KNOW I'M DYING" 46
JEANE 48
A QUIET MAN SPEAKS 53
A TRIBUTE TO A WIFE AND MOTHER 55
BERNARDA 59
A YOUNG MAN 63
THE BOOK OF LIFE 65
I TAKE IT BACK 68
MY BROTHER 71
BERTHA 75
VON 78
A LESSON LEARNED 82
TAKE JESUS' HAND 86
THE MESSAGE 91
THE FIRST DAY OF THE WEEK 93

THE BEGINNING

I delight to do Your will, O my God, and Your law is within my heart.
Psalm 40:8

Life is challenging for all of us at times. I was going through one of those periods. I needed to go back to work and prayed the Lord would guide me in the right direction. Banking had been my career, but for several reasons I could not re-enter that field. At the time, I was volunteering two days a week at the hospital. I enjoyed that very much.

One night I had a dream. In the dream I was walking down a hallway in the hospital. I passed a closed door that read PASTORAL CARE.
What is Pastoral Care? I wondered.
I felt I had not been down that hallway before. The next morning I thought about the dream, trying to remember if I had seen that door before. I did not think I had.

As things go, I forgot about the dream until about three weeks later when indeed I was sent on an errand while volunteering at the hospital. I turned a corner and began to walk down a hallway and there it was, "the door." Just like in the dream it read PASTORAL CARE. I started to shake inside a bit and my heart was beating fast, but I decided to be brave and walk in. There was a woman sitting at a desk inside the door. She smiled and asked if she could help me.
I said, "Yes. What is Pastoral Care and what do you do?"
She replied there was someone in the office who could answer all my questions.

I met the nun who taught CPE (Clinical Pastoral Education). She was happy, vivacious, and patiently answered all my questions. She explained to me that

Pastoral Care was a group of chaplains who visited the patients and families. They were present when patients were critical and dying. She also explained the education that was required to be a chaplain. As we talked, I became excited. This was something I could do to serve the Lord.

I asked if my qualifications were sufficient to begin the CPE class. I swallowed hard and told her about the dream I had had, the life circumstance I was going through, and my desire to do something to serve the Lord. She smiled gently with understanding and we agreed to meet again to discuss my attending the CPE class that was to start in a few weeks. I was on cloud nine. I felt this was the Lord calling me to the ministry of caring for the sick and dying. For the first time in a long time, I felt at peace.

One day Sister called me and said the class might have to be cancelled because there were not enough students.

"No Sister," I said. "We have to pray. God will send the students."

He did. We had five people for that summer class.

CPE was hard. I learned many things about myself and the life circumstance I was going through. My walk with the Lord became closer and I learned to accept my own death. It is difficult to help others if you cannot do this. I thought of my father's death a few years before and drew strength from that experience. Was I scared? Yes. But I knew the Lord would be walking beside me all the way. I attended four units of CPE.

As the years have passed not only has He walked beside me, He has allowed people to share their experiences with me as they are dying. I cannot find words to explain how this makes me feel, but as you read the stories I think you will understand what I am trying to say. You will feel it too.

Some of the families asked me to write the stories in a book. I prayed about it and felt the Lord also wanted me to write them down. I am not a writer. I felt like Moses.

Not me Lord, surely not me!

I dragged my feet. I put it off several years, finding excuses not to begin.

Then one day, when I was praying, I heard that quiet voice in my head I have learned to recognize.

"You help other people get to know Me and teach them to follow My will and be obedient, but you are being disobedient."

I felt afraid.

"How did I disobey You, Lord?"

"I told you to write the book. You have not."

Then I felt ashamed. He was right. I had used every excuse not to begin. My heart knew the right words would come when writing the book. It was time to begin.

MY FATHER'S DEATH—MY FIRST

And let us run with endurance the race that is set before us.
Hebrews 12:1

My father had Alzheimer's for ten years before he died. It was a long journey for my mother and our family. We all faced it differently. It was very difficult seeing a strong man, a German disciplinarian who found it hard to show his love for us outwardly, fail inch by inch and lose control of mind and body.

I did not doubt his love for me, but I'm sure my siblings would tell you it was different for me because I held the esteemed position of being the "baby of the family." My nickname was "After Thought"! My parents had six children.

As I grew older I began telling people, "There were five and then there was me."

Six years divide my brother and me. I'm sure he disliked giving up the position of being the youngest when I was born.

As my father's disease progressed we tried to take turns helping my mother care for him. Mom had heart trouble and the doctor told us she had to be careful. They lived in a senior high rise which made things somewhat easier. Eventually Dad's condition changed and we could not care for him. The doctor recommended we place him in a nursing home where he would get twenty-four hour care. After fifty some years of marriage, Mom was not ready to give up. The doctor insisted, for her health.

I took Mom to visit Dad twice a day at the beginning. Her doctor soon put a stop to that and told her she was to visit once a week. We went once a day. Did I mention I come from a stubborn family?

Dad came to the point of not knowing who we were. This hurt my mother, but she was a strong woman, accepted it, and continued to visit every day.

I must tell you a cute story that happened during this time in the nursing home. Several times Mom and I could not find Dad when we arrived at the home. Each time we found him with the girl in charge of activities. My father had always told my mother during their marriage he did not like blondes. This young girl had beautiful long blonde hair. We would watch him as he followed her everywhere she went. Finally Mom could not take anymore.

Even though Dad could not understand, she said to him one day, "Well, Reynold, you told me you didn't like blondes. I always suspected you were jilted by a blonde before we met!"

A few days after this happened my mother was able to laugh about it. We always knew where to look for Dad if he was not in his room.

Toward the end Dad declined quickly. Other health problems began to arise. The nursing home sent him to the hospital to be checked out, but he returned with the diagnosis "nothing more could be done." Soon after he went into a coma.

Our family spent a lot of time over the next thirty-six to forty-eight hours at his bedside, sometimes taking turns, sometimes many of us together. We would sit around his bed with our mother and talk about old times—good and bad. I noticed when we talked about the bad times he would become restless. During the good stories and our funny stories he would become calm.

This was my first experience of death first hand. I watched Dad's breathing. It was as though he was running a race. I remember thinking it was like he was running up hill to get to Heaven.

The day Dad died it was my turn to sit with him in the afternoon by myself. I was afraid. Of what, I was not sure, but I had a feeling of panic come over me as I sat alone with him. Then I started to talk, not knowing if he could hear me. I told him how much I loved him and thanked him for being my "Pop." That was my favorite name for him. I apologized for the times I caused him distress and told him some things I had done that I didn't think he knew about. I'm sure he knew, but it felt good getting them off my chest. Calmness and peace began to come over me. The panic left.

That evening the family began to arrive one by one. Someone brought Mom after her much needed rest. I took a break and walked up and down the hall outside Dad's room. The evening nurse came up to me and started to talk.

"I just lost my Dad too," she said. "He was playing golf with his buddies. They went to get something to eat and drink afterwards and he just fell over at the table from a heart attack. They could not revive him. I didn't get to say good-bye. You have watched your father slowly die for ten years with Alzheimer's. I don't know which is worse."

She went on to say, "When your father dies he will not be able to speak but he will wake up and know you. Tell him anything you want to. He will be able to hear you."

We hugged each other and I went back to the room. As I said, this was my first death. I had listened to every word she said.

About an hour later, dad's breathing began to change. It slowed.

I thought, *His race is about over.*

Suddenly he opened his eyes and looked at my mother sitting beside his bed. His eyes were brilliant, not like earthly eyes. We could see the love that passed between my mother and father in that look. She told him how much she loved him. As the look continued, Mom looked younger. Her wrinkles disappeared. Then Dad looked at each one of us individually as we stood around the bed. He was saying good-bye to each of us with those brilliant, heavenly eyes.

When his eyes came to me I was able to say, "I love you, Pop."

It was difficult to speak with those brilliant eyes looking directly into my eyes. When he had completed the circle, he looked back at my mother and closed his eyes for the last time and took his last breath. There was silence in the room for a time. We all knew we had experienced something very special and beautiful. This was when I began the belief that death can be beautiful. I feel this was where I was born to be a chaplain, only I did not discover that until years later.

As we were leaving the nursing home after Dad died, the nurse came up to me to give me another hug.

This time she said, "I don't know why I told you those things earlier. I have never experienced a death like your father's before."

I smiled through my tears and said, "God told you to tell me."

What a beautiful gift God gave our family that night. Through the years of being a chaplain and being present when many patients have died, I have never experienced another death like my father's. I feel privileged to be called to do this work and to give comfort like the nurse gave me when my father died. It has been a wonderful journey.

PASS IT ON!

"By this all will know that you are My disciples, if you have love for one another."
John 13:35

During the time I have been a Chaplain, God has given me awesome experiences. I say the over-used word, "Awesome," because I have not found an appropriate word in the English language to describe them. The experiences I speak of are the times I am present with people when they "Walk to the Other Side."

These stories started years ago when I first became a Chaplain. One of the first experiences I remember was the death of a man my age. I was in my early forties at the time. When becoming a Chaplain, you must learn to accept your own death before you can truly help others. I thought I had accomplished this task until I became acquainted with this man and his wife. Almost immediately we bonded as they shared their life story with me. His diagnosis was heart failure from overeating. He was a foodaholic and had been a very large man. Now he was very thin but he retained the excess skin from the past weight gain. They were very open about how he waited too late to save his body, but wanted to be an example to help others if he could.

Through their struggles they both worked on anger. His anger was at himself for overeating and destroying his body. Her anger was directed at him for overeating and not being able to stop in time to live to an old age together. They attended Al-a-non and reached a place of peace and forgiveness. Peace with God and peace and forgiveness with each other.

As the patient declined, I realized he was rapidly approaching death. All of a sudden I felt weak and began to question if I could help this patient and his wife as he died. Then I remembered the promise Jesus made in Matthew 28:20, "Lo, I am with you always, even to the end of the age." God would be with this couple, and God would be with me. Together all of us would make it through.

On the day he was dying, I was called to his bedside.

As I walked into the room, he smiled his usual big grin and said softly, "It's time."

His wife arrived and together we read passages from the Bible together, prayed, and sang. Throughout this time the patient was very peaceful.

As the last minutes approached, I asked the Lord to give him a peaceful death, strength for his wife to carry on without her husband, and courage for me to give them comfort and support during this time.

I leaned down and whispered into the patient's ear, "Jesus loves you."

He gave us one last smile and said, "Yes, I know He does. Pass it on!"

TWO ANGELS

"Likewise, I say to you, there is joy in the presence of the angels of God over one sinner who repents."
Luke 15:10

One morning as I reached the office, a certain patient's name kept coming to my mind. I felt I needed to call his home. When his wife answered the phone she said she was just getting ready to call me.

"Last evening something happened," she excitedly stated. "We want to tell you about it but not over the phone. Can you come?"

"Of course." I said.

As I knocked on the door and entered the living room, I saw the patient sitting in his recliner. His little dog was curled up on his lap but jumped down to greet me. I hugged the patient and his wife and settled on the edge of the hospital bed placed in front of the picture window. The patient began to tell his story.

The night before, his sister-in-law was visiting their home. Suddenly the dog began to bark. The patient looked up and saw two angels standing in the middle of the living room.

"One angel had horns and hooves," the patient said as he looked steadily in my eyes. "The other was a good angel. My wife and sister-in-law could not see the angels, but the dog was standing and barking right where they were standing. I know he could see them. They were fighting over my soul."

He continued. "Jesus will win. Jesus will always win, but we have to pray."

Needless to say, this took my breath away. In fact, I felt chills run down my spine. The patient was very lucid and mentally stable. He was not on any medication that would make him hallucinate.

All I could say was, "Yes, we have to pray."

The patient's wife was sitting on a foot stool close to the patient while he was relating the story. The three of us joined hands to pray. The little dog came up to the foot stool. Standing on his hind legs he put his front paws on the stool and crossed them. The dog kept this position the entire time we prayed. When we finished and I said, "Amen," he got down. Again, it took my breath away. The patient looked around the room and then looked at his wife and me.

"There is only one angel left," he said, "and that is the good angel."

He settled back in his chair and smiled peacefully.

No one will believe this! I thought.

Should I tell this story to our Director and staff? I received my answer as I was leaving their home. The wife walked me to the door and stopped me before going out.

"You have to tell this story," she confirmed. "God wants you to tell people."

I had my answer. Did I have the courage to carry it out was the question. However, before I close this story read on to the next chapter. It continues.

MY MOTHER IN HEAVEN

For instruction in righteousness, that the man (woman) of God may be complete, thoroughly equipped for every good work.
2 Timothy 3:16-17

The patient continued to look at me as he sat in his chair. I could feel there was more on his mind. His wife looked at him puzzled. Also feeling that he had something more to say. Something he had not shared with her. We were correct on all counts.

"There's something more I want to tell you, but you won't believe me," the patient stated.

"Tell me," I said. "I'll believe you."

"No, you won't," he bantered back.

"Yes I will. You can tell me anything," I replied.

After sharing the experience of the two angels and the dog joining us during prayer, I felt ready to hear more. However, I was not ready for his next words.

"I met your mother."

Immediately tears began to flow down my face. I could picture my dear sweet mother with her beautiful smile. How I missed her. She had died eight years before.

"Is she alright?" I asked.

"Oh yes, she is just fine. She took me all over Heaven and introduced me to all kinds of people."

This sounded like my mother. She never knew a stranger. In our small town in Illinois everyone knew her, and she was always doing things for others.

"She took me up on a hill and showed me the throne of God. I could not see God, only His throne," he continued. "It was surrounded by thousands and thousands of angels as far as we could see. They were singing and praising God. The music was like nothing you hear here on earth."

He was painting a picture of Heaven, and it was beautiful.

"Your mother is a teacher."

This was the first time I had a feeling of doubt. My mother had only finished the fifth grade. Her job was to stay with her sisters and sisters-in-law as they had their babies. She cared for the older children and helped with the house work. I shared this with the patient. He looked up in consternation.

Then he said, "Well, maybe not a teacher exactly, but I know this. She is in charge of a large group of children. She watches over them until their families come to heaven."

This also sounded like my mother, watching over the children. There were six of us, and we all brought our friends home. Mom listened to their problems and ours too, plus the grandchildren's.

I was confused, doubting, and hopeful all at the same time.

Finally I asked the patient, "How did you know it was my Mother?"

The patient put his hands on his hips and leaned forward a couple of inches from my face and stated firmly, "Because she told me!"

God knew my doubts. He sees into our hearts and minds.

I heard a voice clearly say in my mind, "This is Heaven. Anything can happen in Heaven."

I asked forgiveness and told the Lord I would not doubt again if a patient shared their experiences with me. I feel it is a special privilege when this happens. Thankfully, I have had many more experiences after this one.

MY MOTHER'S DEATH

"Well done, My good and faithful servant."
Matthew 25:23

My mother and I always had a close relationship. I think that was because I was born so far behind the other children. She was my playmate and she had the patience of Job with me.

On laundry day we would take the clothes basket outside to hang it on the line to dry. Mom would bring out a chair and let me put the clothes pins on each piece. Then she would move the chair and we would hang another item. Do you see what I mean about patience?

Mom and I continued that closeness, even through the teen years and beyond. She had a series of mini strokes in her later years, which caused some dementia. Even during that period I felt she was my support.

Three years before Mom died I met my husband, Jay. We lived in different states. Occasionally I would take him to visit her. She would take his hand and walk him up and down the nursing home halls, announcing to everyone that he was her boyfriend. She would look back at me following them and give me that wonderful smile with her eyes sparkling. It was a joy to see her enjoy herself, even if it was at my expense.

Once when I was visiting her alone and her mind was clear she told me how much she loved Jay.
"He's a good man. Now I can die in peace. I know you will be taken care of," she said.

The inside of me was screaming, *No, I don't want you to die,* but I knew she was getting tired and the strokes were taking their toll. One year before Mom died Jay and I were married.

One of my brothers lived in the town where Mom was in the nursing home. He visited her often. He told me one day he entered her room and she was standing looking out the window.

As she turned she said, "There will be leaves on the ground when it happens."

He knew she meant her death. She also told him about two or three weeks before she died that she had seen Dad standing by the gate waving for her to come. It was fall, and the leaves were on the ground. It was almost time.

My husband and I drove the five hour drive after receiving a call from the nursing home that my mother was dying. About two and a half hours into the journey, we stopped to call the nursing home and inquire how Mom was doing. The nurse reported she was holding her own, and that when they told her I was on the way, she rallied a little. About a half hour after this phone call I felt heaviness come over me, then emptiness. I started to cry.

My husband patted my hand and said, "She will wait for you, Ellen. They said she rallied when she heard you were on your way. Everything will be all right."

I said through my tears, "No Jay, my mother just died. I can feel it."

As we arrived in the small town in Illinois and entered the parking lot of the nursing home I saw all my brothers' cars.

My husband said, "See Ellen, they are all here. Your mother is still alive."

"No Jay, they are just waiting for me to get here."

One of my brothers was standing at the door, looking out waiting for us to arrive and tell us the news. My mother had died at the time I felt the emptiness. But she had come to say, "Good-bye." I did not realize what a gift it was until later.

When I found out my mother had died before I got there, I was angry at God. I was a Chaplain. Why couldn't I be there when she died? After much prayer and thought I realized God's gift to my brothers and my sister was their presence with her as she crossed to the other side. My gift was a beautiful smile on her face that stayed permanently. She was beautiful when I walked into the room. The smile, the look of peace, the look of beauty with no wrinkles left on her face. There was a presence in the room that I will never forget—it was God's presence. It enfolded me. I felt like God was holding me in His arms, giving me comfort but at the same time telling me, "Your mother is mine now. I will take care of her for eternity."

Everyone allowed me to be with my mother alone for as long as I wanted. I sat by her bed side for about an hour, talking to her, telling her how much I loved her, thanking her for being a great mother, and yes, just like when my Dad died I thanked her for putting up with me during my "difficult" times of growing up. My husband knew just when to come back into the room.

I knew God had nudged him and said, "It is time for Ellen to let her go."

Mother had planned her funeral years before. We knew what songs to sing at the funeral, what she wanted to wear, and grandsons were to be the pall bearers. She said she wanted it to be a celebration. This was years before we began to call it a Celebration of Life.

"You can cry, but then have a good time just being together," she had said.

We followed her instructions as best we could.

My husband, children, and I were the first to arrive at the funeral home the night of the visitation. The Funeral Director, whom I've known since I was born, greeted us with a serious look on his face.

He said, "Ellen, there's something I have to tell you."

I could not imagine what it could be. He led me into the room where my Mother lay.

He said, "I could not take that beautiful smile off her face. It is set there forever."

I cried, but I was at peace.

My mother's visitation was a large one. People lined up on the sidewalk outside the funeral home on that cold November evening waiting to get in.

As they filed past my mother's casket we could hear them say, "Why she's smiling!"

It was my Mother's last gift for everyone to see. We knew when she died she was smiling because she saw Dad again, but most of all because she met Jesus face to face for the first time. It was a witness of her faith and a comfort to us. We will always remember that smile.

EIGHT O'CLOCK

"Remember how short my time is."
Psalm 89:47

Many times I have heard stories of people telling someone when they were going to die. My first experience of this happening was when I was working on the cancer floor at the hospital years ago.

While visiting my patient one day, he told me he knew he was going to die at eight o'clock the next morning and would I please be with him. I assured him I would be honored to be present. He stated he was not afraid, but was looking forward to being with the Lord and seeing what Heaven was like. He shared many thoughts and feelings about his life and his family. His wife had died, and no one lived close, except one son. This evening he planned to tell his son what he felt about his dying, and ask him also to be present.

His son and I arrived about 7:00 AM. The patient looked comfortable and at peace about what he felt was about to happen. The 8:00 o'clock hour came and went. The patient cried and became upset.

He said, "I saw the clock and it said 8:00. I don't understand."

He apologized for keeping his son from his work and for getting me up so early. We both tried to comfort him. I visited him often throughout the day and each time he had that puzzled and disappointed look on his face. I was sorry when my shift ended and I had to leave him.

The next morning when I arrived on the floor, one of the nurses was waiting for me.

She said, "Our patient died last night. He was right, it was 8:00 o'clock, but it was PM instead of AM."

The vision the patient experienced was correct. It said 8:00 o'clock. But the clock did not say morning or evening. The patient automatically thought it was to be in the morning.

I like to picture this man entering Heaven with a big smile on his face when he realized that it was indeed God's perfect timing for him to be called home to Heaven at 8:00 o'clock. Only it was 8:00 o'clock in the evening, not 8:00 o'clock in the morning.

"I WANT TO GO HOME"

"For man goes to his eternal home."
Ecclesiastes 12:5

One day a family called me to come and visit with their mother.
"She is talking out of her head and we thought you might be able to straighten her out."
"What is she saying?" I asked.
"She keeps saying that she wants to go home, and we tell her she is home!"

When I arrived, one of the family members said their mother kept repeating an address they could not understand. It was something like 3258, but they could not understand the street name. I shared with them that their mother could be speaking of going to heaven when she spoke of going "home," and perhaps the 3258 was going to be her new address. The entire family had difficulty digesting this information. It was completely foreign and upsetting to them. I shared some scriptures from Revelations describing Heaven and gave them a Bible to read more. Then I went in to visit with the patient.

This was my third visit with the patient. She was a gentle lady with a deep faith and a love of God. She looked peaceful as she smiled when I entered the room.
"I understand you want to go home."
"Oh yes, I want to go to 3258 _____."
Unfortunately I could not understand the street name she said either. I asked her to repeat it, but still could not understand. It came to me that just maybe we were not supposed to understand the street names of Heaven. Perhaps their street names are a very different language from ours. All I knew was this sweet lady was ready to cross over to the other side.

She looked at me and said, "Do you see that beautiful blue dress hanging on the closet door?"

I turned and looked in the direction she was pointing. Indeed, there was a closet door, but I could not see the beautiful blue dress.

She continued, "That is going to be the dress I will wear when I cross over. It is so beautiful."

I shared with her the family's concern about her wanting to go home.

She gave me that quiet peaceful smile and said, "But you understand don't you?"

"Yes," I replied. "You want to go to Heaven and be with the Lord."

She continued, "Please help my family understand, and tell them about the blue dress."

She also asked for prayer for her children and their families. She shared concerns she had for them after she was gone. We prayed together, and then I went to visit with the family again.

We talked about Heaven being a large city with many streets and many people. I told them about her blue dress. I told them how much she loved them and would miss them, but that she wanted to go home now to be with the Lord, and join their father who had died years before. Some began to understand, some did not.

Their mother died the next day. She looked so beautiful and I could picture her in her new blue dress in heaven meeting God for the first time. You could feel the peace in the room, and I hope I transferred that peace in a small way to each family member as I hugged them after their mother left her earthly home for the last time.

CAN I BRING HER WITH ME?

Precious in the sight of the Lord is the death of His saints.
Psalm 116:15

This was the first time since I came to work at Hospice that we had a husband and wife on service at the same time. Their bedroom was large and there was plenty of room for all of their medical equipment, oxygen, and beds.

Both enjoyed telling our staff stories about their life, their family and their work, especially the husband. He had been in a management position, and had a wealth of knowledge about organization and finance, which he shared with us freely. He also had a wonderful sense of humor, and loved telling jokes and stories.

The wife declined first, and it was hard for the husband to watch, but he refused to be moved to another room. They had been together many years and they were not about to be separated now. She died quietly one night in her sleep. Her husband woke early to find she had gone before him. He grieved but stated he knew it would not be long before God would call him home too, and he would be with her again.

A couple of months later he also started to decline. This was hard on the family, because of just losing their mother. The patient continued to keep his sense of humor, however, having at least one joke or story to tell our staff each time they visited.

One night the Hospice Nurse phoned for me to come. The patient was restless and was asking for me. When I arrived he kept getting in and out of bed. I tried to speak with him and pray with him to comfort him and the family.

Suddenly he began to speak to someone the rest of us could not see.

He said to that person, "Yes, I'm ready to go."

Then he took the white top sheet off the bed and wrapped it around his body and asked, "Is this what I should wear?"

At the time I was standing beside the patient with the nurse on the other side holding him up because of his weakness. His family was close by. He looked at me and smiled and reached for another white sheet and wrapped it around me.

Then he looked at the person we could not see and asked, "Can I bring her with me? She is dressed ready to go."

Everyone gasped, and waited for what would happen next.

I must confess my heart was beating fast. I felt many emotions.

I was touched that the patient wanted me to go to heaven with him, but the human side of me said, *Wait, I'm not sure I want to go yet!*

In my heart I knew God would direct what was to transpire.

The patient continued to look at the person we could not see, and then hung his head and asked, "She can't come with me? Oh."

Everyone seemed to breathe a sigh of relief, including me. His family came to hold him and comfort him, while the nurse and I remade the bed and coaxed the patient to lie down. I held his hand and a short time later he went to sleep and then entered into a coma. The next day he died.

That was an awesome experience for everyone that night, especially for the family losing two parents so close together. We all discussed the things we had heard and seen. We wondered who the person was the patient spoke to. Even though God did not want me to come with him, I know it was someone God sent to walk him across to the other side, and he was not alone on that journey to the other side.

A LOVE STORY

Where has your beloved gone, that we may seek him with you?
Song of Solomon 6:1

Early one Saturday morning I received a call from one of our Hospice nurses. She told me some shocking news. One of our patients had just died and her husband had died a short time before her, less than an hour and a half between them. He had died of an apparent heart attack.

This couple had been married sixty-five years. They had nine children, one of which I had worked with a few years before. They were a close knit family. The children, their spouses, and grandchildren took turns taking care of this sweet couple. The family support was wonderful to observe.

The patient started to decline about a week before she died. I had the opportunity to visit with them both at that time.

As we visited the husband stood by her bedside, stroked her face and said, "I love you very much."

The husband shared how he would miss his wife and that he wanted to go with her. Looking back, that was our first indication of what was to come. Many couples who have been married a long time have this desire and ask the Lord for this to happen. Sometimes God grants their wish.

After I visited the couple, I stopped at the nursing home where the daughter I knew worked to give her support and a hug. I told her I had seen her graduation picture on the living room wall and thought we were the same age.

When I told my age to her sister-in-law during the visit, I soon found out my friend was a few years younger than I. Knowing how this family likes to kid, I knew if I did not tell my friend myself about the age mistake, the story would get blown all out of proportion.

We laughed about it and reminisced about our bouffant hair we wore in those days.

Then she told me how a day or two before she was kidding her mother that she was the pretty one in the family, and her one sister, who was just driving in the driveway was the ugly one. She said her mother promptly scolded her and told her to behave.

Even though their mother was ill, she could still tell them what to do and keep them in line. As I mentioned before, this family loved to tease one another.

When I arrived at the patients' home the morning they died, the family and nurse shared the events of the last three days. Two days before the patient died, she asked her girls to call the boys to come.

She said, "I've been talking to the Lord."

Then she said, "Go get your Dad. I'm on the road to Heaven and he can go with me if he wants to."

Without anyone knowing it, this was another indication of what was going to happen.

The Hospice nurse made a visit to the patient the day before she died. The nurse spoke to the husband about telling his wife it was alright to go to be with the Lord. He said he had "sort of" told her it was OK.

The nurse encouraged him to speak with her again. They helped him to a chair right beside the bed and everyone left them alone to talk together.

As the nurse was leaving the room she looked back and witnessed the most beautiful and awesome look pass between the couple. She said it was almost a heavenly look. It appeared the patient was seeing right through to her husband's soul. I'm sure sixty-five years of love was shown in that look.

The husband gently stroked his wife's face and told her how much he loved her. The couple talked for awhile. What they said to each other will never be known. This may have been the time they discussed and prayed to the Lord about going to Heaven together.

Many family members stayed the night. They began to stir about at 4:00AM. Then they heard their father ring his bell and knew he was in trouble. He seldom rang his bell for help. They helped him all they could, but he died shortly after.

One of the girls told their mother that he had died, but was not sure she heard or understood, because she was in a coma and in the dying process herself. I think she heard and I think she knew.

I can picture him saying to her, "Come on Mom, it is time to go. We will go together. The Lord said it was all right."

Time and time again, I have seen where God speaks to dying people and lets them know ahead of time what is to happen. Often they share their wishes with their family or the Hospice staff.

Also, sometimes they have conversations with the Lord and their loved ones who have gone before. Not all the time, but it does happen. This couple's desire was to go to Heaven together. God granted their request.

It was very hard on the family in many ways, but in other ways they were rejoicing their parents were still together. They shared life stories about when they were young and teased each other about some of them.

One brother teased, "Mom said I was the best looking!"

We talked about the wedding vows we pledge when we get married, "Till death do us part." Death parted them from this earth, but they left this earth together and are in Eternity together forever. It was a beautiful love story.

A COUNTRY GRAVESIDE SERVICE

Suddenly there came up out of the (field) cows, fine looking and fat, and they fed in the meadow.
Genesis 41:2

We drove in procession to a beautiful little cemetery in the country for the graveside service. It was a sunny day, but cold. Across the road from the cemetery was a huge pasture. You could see the cows grazing. As the hearse pulled into the cemetery along with all of the other cars, I could see the cows begin to move toward the fence, but did not think anything about it.

As the service was about to begin, I saw the cows had come up to the fence, side by side in rows, looking across to the cemetery. I thought how strange it was. It looked as though they were standing at attention and in some way a part of the ceremony. The family, also, was looking at the cows across the road as I began the service.

The patient had not been on Hospice very long and I had asked the family to tell me about him so I could share some of their stories. Apparently they forgot to tell me everything.
As I was speaking, the family continued to glance across to the pasture and one by one they began to laugh. I was puzzled but continued the service.
At the end I stated, "This concludes the service."
Do you know what happened? The cows began to disperse!

By this time everyone was laughing. A family member came up to me and began to apologize for the laughter.

"One of the things we forgot to tell you about Dad was that he was a cattle broker during part of his life. It seemed so fitting for those cows to be standing in rows, watching and saying, 'We're still here and you are not!'"

Humor helped them through the day. At the dinner after the service many told the story over and over again.

I could understand the cows coming in a group watching us, but the standing in rows is a mystery.

It is also a mystery why they stood at attention until I said, "This concludes the service."

This story I will never forget.

"TELL THEM TO SING"

Speaking to one another in psalms and hymns and spiritual songs, singing and making melody in your heart to the Lord.
Ephesians 5:19

I was called one night to go sit with a patient and her family as she was dying. The patient was restless. I sat beside the bed, holding her hand, talking to her and praying with them.

We shared many things that night. We talked about the Lord and His love for us. Each of the four children shared some of their life experiences and stories about their family as they were growing up.

The patient grew quieter as they talked. I know she was following each story even though she could not respond or speak.

Even though she began to be peaceful it seemed she was waiting for something or someone. I asked if all of the family had been to visit her so she could say their good-byes. They said all of the grandchildren had come and they all had told her it was all right for her to go be with Jesus.

Still something remained unfinished.

I prayed for the Lord to show us what was needed and heard a voice in my head say, "Tell them to sing."

When I repeated this to the children they gasped. They told me they had begun singing together in church when they were young. They sang for many years, stopping only when the first one got married and moved away. They had not sung together since. I asked them if they would sing for their mother now.

The music and harmony were beautiful. The singing was soft and quiet at first but picked up volume as they continued to sing. Anyone listening could not tell it had been years since they had sung together.

Their mother became restful and peaceful and her breathing became slower. The children stopped and looked at each other.

One said, "Should we sing Mom's favorite Gospel song?"

Another said, "Yes."

They began to sing softly. You could feel the peace in the room. Their mother's breathing became slower and slower. When they finished the last verse, she drew her last breath.

It was beautiful. This was what she was waiting for, hearing her children sing one last time and singing her into Heaven.

They recorded the song for the funeral because they did not think they could get through it at the Service. As the song was played I could picture their mother looking down with the Lord smiling, and the Lord telling her what a good job she had done raising her children.

It was comforting for the children to spend those last hours with their mother, sharing stories and singing for her one last time before she died.

THE ANGEL MAN

For He shall give His angels charge over you, to keep you in all your ways.
Psalm 91:11

Shortly after I became a Hospice chaplain I was asked to accompany one of the nurses to meet a man that was to become one of my patients. I was told he had been seeing angels and I was most anxious to speak with him about this. The feeling was not mutual.

This patient had been in the military for several years and when he was told the new chaplain was a woman stated, "Chaplains are supposed to be men."

The nurse asked if she could bring me, "just once," to meet him and his wife. Then if they did not want me to return, I would not.

Needless to say I was nervous as we entered their home. As we sat visiting, I could tell they were nervous too, but soon we all began to relax and visit.

When the visit was over he stated in his military voice, "You can come again."

I smiled as we got into the car and prayed, *Thank you, Lord.*

It was a very hot summer that year and I was in the middle of putting up with the "power surges" that come with middle age.

The patient was always cold, but when he would see me drive into the driveway, he would call to his wife, "Ma, she's here. Put the fan on."

Then the visit would begin.

On each visit I sat on the sofa, the patient in his recliner, and the wife in her rocking chair with a foot stool.

The wife told me that every time the patient knew I was coming, he would insist on wearing his new burgundy pajamas that I had complimented him about, and, have his hair combed just right.

Then he would sit and wait for me to arrive.

On my second visit he began to tell me about his Angels.

"I have two," he stated proudly. "One is a white man and the other is a black woman," he described.

Then he continued, "They give me a lot of comfort at night when I am in pain and can't sleep."

His wife shared she would ask them for guidance during the night when the patient was having trouble. Then suddenly an idea of something that would help him would come into her mind, and it would work. She was positive the Angels gave her the help.

During a visit in late June I was sitting in my normal spot visiting with the patient and his wife. He kept looking at the space on the sofa beside me. I followed his glance. There was nothing there.

Sometimes their little dog would curl up beside me while we visited, but on this day he had stayed outside. The patient was not looking at him, I thought.

He looked there again and said, "Ellen, there's an Angel sitting beside you."

I looked quickly at the space to catch a glimpse of this Angel. I could see nothing.

Then he said, "Ellen, all of your grandchildren are blond aren't they?"

You could have picked me up off the floor. Yes, my grandchildren are all blond. I have dark brown hair, almost black.

My mind raced. *How could he have known this?*

Up to this point I had not shared about my grandchildren.

"How did you know that," I asked

Softly I heard a voice in my head say, "Ellen, I told the angel to tell him that so you would believe."

I felt it was the Lord's voice.

God knew the doubts I had when the patient told me about the angels. I thought he had been watching too much of the television program *Touched by An*

Angel that was popular at the time when he said one was a white man and the other was a black woman.

Did I feel ashamed? Yes. Did I ask God for forgiveness? Also, yes.

After looking at the space beside me again the patient said, "Ellen, the angel sitting beside you is your angel. It is your guide and your protector."

I felt warm all over and this time it was not a power surge. It was God hugging me. I could feel His love. These words came to me.

An angel sat beside me today,
Oh, what a wonderful feeling!
He said the angel was my guide and protector,
I feel so loved by God.

I began to ask many questions.
"Is my angel a man or a woman?"
"A man with long blond hair parted on the left side."
"What is he wearing?"
"A white robe with a gold rope tied around his waist."
"What does he look like?"
"I never told you, Ellen, I cannot see the angels' faces. I can tell what color skin they have and if they are a man or woman, but I can't see their faces. But when I get close to being called home to Heaven I feel I will be able to see their faces."
"What is his name?"
After he looked at the space beside me for awhile he replied, "I can't tell you now. Later I will find out and tell you then."

And he did.
Several visits later he said his angels told him my angel's name. It was Andrew. I was not ready to hear that on that first day because of thinking he was watching too much *Touched by an Angel*.

But, today I believed in the angels and was pleased with my angel's name.

Andrew is a special name to me. Both of my grandfather's names were Andrew.

Also, a cousin who was ten years older than me was named Andrew and he had blond hair. He died at a young age from cancer leaving a wife and several children.

I had been close to Andy even though we had the ten years age difference. Thinking of all these "Andrews" gave me comfort.

"Do you think my angel would mind if I called him Andy?" I asked.

The patient looked at the space close to me where my angel was, then smiled and answered, "He wouldn't mind a bit."

Often I thought of our conversations about the angels and how God had revealed the fact that my grandchildren were blond.

I shared with this couple there was going to be another grandchild in March. The patient could not wait until the baby was born and see what color the baby's hair would be.

On March 23rd of that year a beautiful baby girl with very blond hair was born.

As winter progressed the patient told me of speaking to Gabriel and Michael the Archangel.

Sometimes he would tell me the angels were speaking about me the night before.

I always asked what they said, and each time he would just smile and say, "Can't tell you, Ellen."

One day he said, "I've been walking in the garden with the Lord some nights."

I felt privileged he was sharing this information with me.

"What do you talk about," I asked.

He gave me the smile I was getting used to and repeated, "Can't tell you, Ellen. Can't tell you."

Then one visit he said, "Ellen, I have a message for you from Jesus."

I felt awed, overwhelmed, and scared all at the same time.

He continued.

"First of all, Jesus wants you to know that you are doing what God the Father wants you to do, help people to walk to the other side."

Again, I felt the warmth of God's love and I was thankful for His guidance.

"Jesus said the Father assigns a guardian angel to each of us. If we feel we need more protection for ourselves or for our families we can ask for it, only we must ask the Father for this protection, not our angel or even Jesus, only God the Father," he stated.

Then he gave me a message for all of you. I will write it at a later time in the book. You will understand why.

The angel man had been reading the Bible through for the fourth time and was in Revelations. He had shared with me he was worried about leaving his family and not being able to take care of them.

He told me he asked Jesus, "When will the world come to an end?"
He said Jesus looked at him with kind gentle eyes and said, "The world ends every day for people when they die."
This does not contradict anything in the Bible, it states a fact put very simply.

Spring arrived and the patient was getting weaker. A daughter arrived from out of state, then a son. Everyone was looking forward to getting together, but the patient was not well enough to speak with them much. He was disappointed and so were they.

Shortly after that visit, the patient told his wife and me he was beginning to see the angel's faces come into focus although they were still blurry. We knew the time was getting near.

Two weeks later I called to check on them and the wife said it was time. I spent a good part of the afternoon sitting at his bedside with her. During that time he spoke his last words to us.
They were, "I see their faces."
He went into a coma shortly after and died peacefully a few hours later.

I cannot tell you how privileged I have felt to have been a part of this man's journey to Heaven.
The messages from the Lord were—well, there are no words in the English language that describes how I feel. Awed does not even touch it.

Many times I have told the story of the Angel Man and the messages he gave me. Almost every time after I speak, people come and share their stories with me. I like that.

I pray it will continue when I share these stories in the future.

LADY, I BELIEVE YOU

And my God shall supply all your need according to His riches in glory.
Philippians 4:19

One Sunday my husband was asked to sing and I was asked to give the message at the Angel Man's church several months after his death. I spoke about the three main stories I usually share.

It felt somewhat strange looking into the faces of the Angel Man's family while I told his story. Some of them had not heard his complete story about the angels and walking with the Lord in the garden before he died. Some smiled as they listened. Some shed a few tears. It was so good seeing his wife again and giving her a big hug.

Several people besides the family lined up to speak to us after the service. One man shared how he had lost a child a short time before. He said the stories gave him comfort and hoped my mother was the person taking care of his child until God called him home to Heaven. Others shared experiences of losing their loved ones and how that had occurred. One young man hung back, shuffling his feet from side to side.

Finally he came up to me and said, "I didn't believe you and your 'nice' stories. I thought they were too good to be true. Then you talked about the two angels, you know, the good one and the bad one. I knew then you were for real. Lady, I believe you. You told both sides: Heaven and Hell."

He walked away without another word.

We never know how and when God will use us. I am thankful God gave me the words to speak on this particular morning to touch this young man in some way in the stories I told. I wonder today what this young man is doing with his life. Is he married and where is he living? Does he have children?

I don't need to know. God knows.

A SENSE OF HUMOR

Nevertheless He did not leave Himself without witness; He gave us rain from heaven, filling our hearts with gladness.
Acts 14:17

One of my first Hospice patients had a great sense of humor. He always had a joke for the staff when we arrived.

He enjoyed showing off his picture window in their living room. A tornado had gone down their street years before and the force of the storm put a tooth pick into the glass. The glass was not broken in any way. It taught all of us as we looked at it to respect Mother Nature.

During our visits the patient shared he wanted his family to smile and remember him fondly when he died. His desire was granted.

Many family and friends were gathered at the cemetery for the graveside service. We were waiting for one more family member to arrive before we started, when I saw something move out of my peripheral vision. It was the casket. The grave was on a slight slope.

People stopped talking and stared. The funeral home staff hurriedly apologized to the family for not securing the casket properly. I watched as they made sure this time it would not move.

The crowd began to talk quietly again, keeping an eye on the casket, while we continued to wait for the family to come. Then the casket moved for the second time. Again, everyone became silent. Again, the funeral home staff apologized and said they were sure it was secured after the first time it moved.

They looked at me for affirmation because I had observed them securing the casket and then rechecking it a second and third time.

One by one the family began to smile. They felt it was their Dad telling them he was alright and playing one last joke on them.

As the minister performed the service I looked around at the family and friends gathered. They had smiles on their faces just the way the patient had wanted.

"PLEASE TELL THEM I KNOW I'M DYING"

Forgetting those things which are behind and reaching forward to those things which are ahead.
Philippians 3:13

Each person and family handles death differently. Many times families have asked our staff not to mention to the patient that we are from Hospice and not to talk about dying. This is difficult. Almost 100% of the time the patient knows they are dying and they want to talk about it, especially with their families. This next story is an example.

The patient was a woman in her early nineties. It was my second visit with the family and, again, they reminded me not to mention dying to the patient. When we entered her room she smiled and asked to speak to me alone. The children looked concerned but complied to her wishes. I could feel their unease.

When the door was shut the patient held her hand out for me to take.
As I took her hand she gently pulled me closer and whispered, "Please tell my family I know I'm dying and I'm OK with it."
She shared more of her feelings about going to Heaven to be with the Lord and how she looked forward to that. She also shared about her health and her pain. Her desire was to be able to speak with all of the children about these subjects. We spoke of the best way to tell them and we prayed about it. Then I went to look for the family.

I didn't have to look far. They were right outside the door.

Taking a deep breath I said, "Your mother wants you to know that she is dying and she is OK with it. She wants to speak with you about it."

There was silence and then deep sighs. Keeping this secret was hard for them too. Having everything out in the open would take stress away.

As we entered the room, there were hugs, tears, and talking all at once. When they settled down each had their say and shared their feelings. It was a healing time for everyone. Now they could spend quality time with their mother and not have to measure their words.

Peace and harmony was restored.

JEANE

There is a time to be born and a time to die, a time to weep and a time to laugh.
Ecclesiastes 3:2, 4

Jeane was one of the most spiritual women I have ever met. She hid it from most people but it was there. When she first came on Hospice she refused a chaplain.
She simply stated, "I don't need one."

One day she was channel surfing and came across the Catholic television station where a nun was leading the rosary. Jeane was not Catholic, but found the repetitious prayers comforting. Since our Hospice is based out of a Catholic hospital, Jeane asked her nurse if she knew how to get a tape of the rosary. Then, she could listen whenever she wanted.

I happened to be a Catholic chaplain and the nurse asked me how to get a tape. I told her one of our nurses had a Rosary tape and could I deliver it to the patient. She said she would ask permission first since Jeane had refused a chaplain. Jeane agreed.

Our relationship began. During our visits, Jeane shared stories of her life. She was quite a lady. We laughed many times as she vividly told of her escapades. She loved Las Vegas, motorcycles, her family, nature, and God. Eventually we had some deep spiritual conversations. I was honored she shared some of her insights with me.

Jeane openly spoke of her death, of going to Heaven, and how all of this was going to affect her family. She had spoken to each family member separately about her cancer. The story that touched me the most was when she spoke to her six year old granddaughter, Lily.

Jeane told her, "Gram has cancer."

Lily replied, "Oh, that's not good."

When Lily went to bed that evening she told her mom about her conversation with Gram.

Then she asked, "Will I get it?"

"No," her Mom said.

"Good," said Lilly.

Then Lilly gave her mother a kiss and a hug, curled up in bed and went to sleep. Children are wonderful and accept things far better than adults, but we have to answer their questions when they ask.

The next thing Jeane did was take Lily on a field trip to the funeral home. She wanted her to feel comfortable when the day came for her funeral and wanted her not to be afraid.

There was a large fish aquarium in the lobby as you enter the building. Lily enjoyed watching the fish and dancing around the aquarium.

Through this experience Jeane taught us a lesson about death and dying. Facing it openly and honestly with her family helped them through the days to come.

In the fall, my husband and I were working on the MDA campaign and met Joy Robertson a news anchor from Channel 10. She asked where I worked. When I said St. John's Hospice Care, she replied she wanted to do a story on death and dying and did I have any patients that might be interested in letting her follow their journey. Immediately, I thought of Jeane. Jeane was a nurse and part of her career she taught in a nursing school in St. Louis. This could be her opportunity to teach a last lesson to everyone.

I asked permission from the hospital to approach Jeane. When it was granted I became nervous. How could I ask someone to share their last journey on television for all to see?

Lord, please help me, I prayed, as I drove to Jeane's home.

Asking Jeane could not have been easier.

Immediately she said, "Yes, I would love to."

"But Jeane, don't you want to ask your family first?"

Her reply was, "No, it's my decision. This will be my last gift to them. Give Joy my number and tell her to call me."

What a woman.

As one would expect, it took Jeane's family longer than Jeane to warm up to the idea of a television journalist following their mother's last journey. Joy met with Jeane and then met Jeane's children and their families. Joy has a way of making everyone feel comfortable as questions are asked. The interviews went well.

Jeane and her family were very honest about their feelings when asked, even when things were not going well.

The series helped people going through the same trials, the trial of dying and the trial of caring for their loved ones. Many shared their feelings with me during the programs and after the series were over. The series helped them realize they were not alone.

Jeane began to decline as the holidays approached.

Everyone knew this would be her last Christmas, especially Jeane. Was she sad? No, she planned a party. Her family was there, also Joy and her two little girls.

They decorated the tree, ate good food, and had a great time. Through all of this you could hear Jeane's laughter and see her smile as she watched everyone having a good time.

This was exactly how she wanted her last Christmas to be, happy and surrounded by family and friends.

On another day close to Christmas, my husband, Jay, and I went to visit Jeane.

She said she wanted to meet Jay before she died and would he sing for her. Joy was there too. We sat in a circle, visited and sang Christmas carols together.

Jay passed inspection and I had to sit there while they talked about me.

The time was getting closer.

People watching the series on TV could see Jeane's decline. We asked her several times if she wanted to stop being filmed.

Each time she replied with a smile on her face, "No, I want to teach people how to die."

During this time Jeane had to have fluid drawn off her stomach two times. She was uncomfortable and in pain.

True to her teaching, she allowed Joy and me to accompany her and her daughter to the hospital and into the procedure room.

The first procedure was successful, the second was not. Tears were shed as we all accepted what this meant.

Jeane's daughters did a wonderful job taking care of her. Kathy took a leave of absence from her work. Susie, a student nurse, kept up a rigorous schedule of school and taking her turn. They moved their families into Jeane's home.

Each had their own way of caring for their mother. They didn't always agree, as they will tell you, but they worked it out between them.

TJ and Melissa, Kathy's two children, helped with the care, along with Donny, Susie's husband, and Miss Lily. We nicknamed the six year old granddaughter Miss Lily because she kept all of us straight and in line.

On one of the television episodes, Joy reported Lily's age incorrectly.

Miss Lily, with finger wagging at the camera, scolded Joy and told the audience, "I am six, not five."

They all had their own specialties when helping with Gram. TJ spent hours staying with Jeane while the girls took a break, Melissa gave wonderful foot messages, Donny ran errands where ever needed, and Miss Lily made Gram microwave oatmeal when it sounded good to her.

All of them had special times just talking to their grandmother about life and things that were important to them.

Two sons and their families lived out of state. They came as often as they could and treasured the time they spent with her.

One weekend most of them came for a work day. Jeane had a great backyard with a gazebo. She wanted landscaping done, but did not get it finished. The family did it for her.

Jeane told me it was a great day watching everyone work so hard and all she had to do was sit and drink coffee.

As the time drew closer, a Hospice volunteer was assigned to give the family extra breaks when they needed it. The volunteer was a young woman who had lost her mother a few months earlier. Jeane and the girls bonded immediately with her. They shared their experiences, laughing and crying together.

One night, Joy called after the news cast, and asked if she could come and hang out with Jeane and the girls. At this point Jeane had her days and nights mixed up. So, into the late night or maybe I should say early morning hours, they all had a gab fest, sharing secrets and stories. Joy filmed some of it.

At one point Jeane looked directly into the camera and said, "If you film that I'll kill you."

All we could hear on television, when it aired, was laughter, leaving everyone wondering what she had shared.

During the last week I stopped in every day, taking my turn sitting with Jeane. Most times she slept, but one day she opened her eyes, looked at me, and smiled.

"What are you smiling at, Jeane?" I asked.

"I just saw my father. He was making popcorn for the kids," she replied.

Then she took my hand, told me she loved me, and said, "I'm ready to go."

Those were some of the last words I had with Jeane.

A day or so later she went into a coma. The family played the rosary tapes and Jeane's favorite music.

The night she died her family, her Hospice nurse, and I were gathered around the bed when she drew her last breath. Joy came as soon as the news was over.

Many tears were shed as we joined hands to say our last goodbyes and to pray. I started the prayer, thanking God for this wonderful lady who taught us how to live to the fullest, and, also, how to die. At that moment Jeane's cat jumped on the bed.

All I could think of to say was, "And now we have the cat on the bed."

Everyone laughed.

Jeane loved to laugh. It was as though she sent the cat to help lighten our moment of saying goodbye. She was still teaching us.

I hope Jeane's story will help you when you are facing the trials of life. Think of how she faced death, head on, with God's help. We prayed together often during her journey. She faced death with humor, but she shed tears, too.

Jeane planned how she wanted things to go. One of her most important lessons she taught us was talking to each family member. Everyone had the opportunity to ask questions and share their feelings with her. It took courage to discuss death openly.

Her daughter, Suzie, said many times about her mother, "You tell her no."

No one refused Jeane when she asked to speak with them about her illness. As they look back, they can see how she made things as easy as could be under the circumstances. Jeane's last lesson continues to be taught.

A QUIET MAN SPEAKS

But let it be the hidden person of the heart, with the incorruptible ornament of a gentle and quiet spirit, which is very precious in the sight of the Lord.
1 Peter 3:4

A man came on Hospice about a year after I began to work there. His wife, an English war bride, told us he was a very quiet man who spoke few words. Our staff found this to be true, but, as the days and weeks passed he began to open up to us. We talked about his favorite subjects, his family and fishing.

I also loved visiting with his wife. She was a delightful lady with a good outlook on life. She loved to walk. Often when our staff visited we encouraged her to do just that and take a break.

The patient began to decline. Our conversations turned to the subjects of God and Heaven and how God sometimes allows a person to see things on the other side before they die.

He said, "I like that idea."

The patient may have been quiet during his lifetime, but he shared with me a deep faith and love of the Lord as he was preparing to die.

One day when I was visiting there was a lull in the conversation. It was not an uncomfortable time, but a peaceful space. We often sat quietly together.

On this day, several times I watched as he glanced to the opposite side that my chair was sitting.

I decided to ask, "What are you seeing? Do you see angels?"

He replied, "Yes, There's one standing right beside me over here."

The patient pointed in the direction he had been glancing. He went on to tell me the angel was with him often and this made him feel comfortable.

The patient also said, "Sometimes there are two angels. I think one is for my wife."

Later I shared this with his wife. She could hardly believe it. Her husband had not spoken about the angels to her and she wondered why.

I told her many times patients speak about things they see on the other side to the Hospice staff, but, do not tell their families about these things. They tell the staff because they are afraid their families will not believe them.

The patient's wife was pleased that the angels made her husband feel comfortable but was disappointed he did not share the story with her.

During the hours before the patient died, I had the opportunity to share the angel story with the patient's son. He, too, was touched the angels made his father feel comfortable and at peace.

I assured him the angels were present during his father's last hours and they would be there to help him walk across to the other side.

A TRIBUTE TO A WIFE AND MOTHER

A wife of noble character who can find? She is worth more than rubies.
Proverbs 31:10

Last week I was called out shortly before midnight. A sixty-four year old woman just died who was on Hospice only a few days. When I arrived there were many tears because the patient had declined rapidly and the family was not prepared.

The husband kept repeating, "I can't believe it, I just can't believe it."

He shared with me how they always did everything together; going to the store, to doctor's appointments…everything. The children said she was the best mom ever.

The next day the funeral home called and said the family would like for me to have the graveside service. I agreed to do this and asked the family to write something about the patient because I had never met her.

Following are some of the most loving tributes I have received to read at a funeral. This was a special lady who was beautiful inside and out and loved by her family…

From her Husband

She was daughter, wife, mother, grandmother, and my best friend. She was always involved with all of us, keeping us in line, on time, and organized. She managed to keep track of all of our appointments, obligations, personal records, and so many other things.

With me, she never gave up on me or ridiculed me, no matter how many mistakes I made or how serious those mistakes might be. She always forgave me, supported me, took care of me, watched my back, and truly loved me like no other person ever has. She was my best friend, and the love of my life. If I am any kind of a man today, it is because of her.

>And now to the end she finally has come
>And her mission in life is finally done
>She can rest with the assurance that we shall be
>Together throughout all Eternity

From the family:

Things Remembered About My Mother

My mother was the matriarch of our family; she was the glue that bonds us together. She was always so concerned about the well being of all of us and always so protective of those needing protection. I will never forget her infectious laugh and how she loved the way I was so animated while I told her of my stories. I love my mother more than words could ever say and I will miss her for all the days of my life. I feel a huge void in my heart and in my life and I pray that I will have that void filled when I see her again.

You Will Be Remembered

You will be remembered each spring as the flowers begin to bloom and in the summer when the lightning bugs light up in the night. You will be remembered in the fall when the leaves begin to change colors and in the winter in the stories that are told. You will always be remembered in my heart.

Mom

Mom meant so much to me and everybody else too. She was the glue that kept everything and everybody together.

Mom was the best mom anybody could ever have in the world. She wasn't just a mom. She was so much more. She did everything and had her hand in everybody's life.

My life would not be the same if she hadn't been in it. So I thank God for her life.

Mom

This woman's life cannot be measured or weighed. It was full of love and strength, when most call it "Woman's Work."

I think of it as a legacy, for it is the very best of her that lives in the hearts of each of us. It is in our family.

We are broken at the loss of her. Our only comfort is that she is no longer suffering. We miss her but know that she will never leave us, for she is here in our hearts always.

Mom

She was the one you've known forever, the one you go to for honest advice and genuine support. The one who accepts your quirky little habits and understood you in a way few others can. You could call her at any hour, to laugh or to cry, even complain—the one whose voice has been there all along, sharing your secrets and your dreams. She would play your favorite song when you needed to hear it most. She could read your mind. I guess she really paid attention when you talked. She would hear your heart and touch it in so many ways, but most off all she would love you just the way you are, and that is why I know she always will be with us in our hearts and spirits.

Tribute

The thing we will remember most is her laughter. Just hearing her laugh would make us laugh too. Our first recollection was at the movies, we can't even remember the movie, but we remember the laughter. She was not worried about what others thought, she was enjoying herself. What a glorious sound. If we close our eyes now, we can hear her laughing. May the tears shed today be not only of sorrow, but of joy. Rejoice knowing that she has been made whole again. May her laughter fill the heavens and our hearts forever.

Until we meet again.

My Beautiful Mom

Special and unique things my mom did or said....It was funny to hear my mom try to say the word aluminum, or whenever she would sneeze she would cross her legs. My mom's little "piggy" toes would cross over the other toe next to it all by itself. I found that to be a unique thing. She was even able to walk like that. She would just laugh about it. Her laughter, sense of humor and smile was some of her beautiful qualities. She had the prettiest hair. As a little girl I loved to comb it. She had a wonderful complexion. My mom would comment, "I'm not as pretty as I used to be." I always told her how wrong she was and that she is "beautiful to me." When playing phone tag with my mom, she would say "hello my daughter, my daughter" and we would joke about me coming over, even after she moved for coffee and visiting on my day off work. When I would not be feeling well I would call my mom. I would tell her how much I wished I was a kid again because she always took good care of us kids. I miss my MOM. I remember one time as a little girl she told me to stay with her in the store or she would spank me in front of God and everyone. I did not believe her but she kept her word. She was spunky, feisty, caring, understanding, and an accepting person. She may not agree with some of our personalities, and she would always tell you, but she accepted you for who or what you were….and loved you! She is loved and graciously remembered for all her special, unique and BEAUTIFUL qualities. God speed to you Mom.

There will be an empty seat at our table, where mom used to sit…but we will be thankful for all she brought to our family table…now there is a seat filled at God's table…where her beauty will be for eternity.

In the prayer card given out at the service the following words appeared. They are perfect for this lady who I got to know through her husband and family.

Afterglow

I'd like the memory of me to be a happy one. I'd like to leave an afterglow of smiles when life is done. I'd like to leave an echo whispering softly down the ways; of happy times and laughing times and bright sunny days. I'd like the tears of those who grieve, to dry before the sun of happy memories that I leave when life is done.

BERNARDA

All the days of her life, she willingly works with her hands. She provides food for her household. She girds herself with strength, and strengthens her arms. And her lamp does not go out by night. She reaches out her hands to the needy. Strength and honor are her clothing. Her children rise up and call her blessed.
Taken from Proverbs 31

One Friday I left work early because it had been a busy week. The Lord had called three people home during the night and evening hours of the days I was on call.

I picked up my husband to go to our favorite pizza place for a quick, early supper. My cell phone rang as we were walking in the door. One of the nurses on my team was on the line. I wondered why she was calling because I knew she was on vacation and had been out of state. I soon found out.

"My mother is in the Emergency Room and it doesn't look good. Can you come?" she asked.

"I'll be there as soon as I can," I replied.

As I entered the room in ER I realized her mother was very critical and appeared to be in the dying process. She turned her face and looked directly into my eyes when she heard my voice.

Bernarda and I had known each other for about eleven years. I met her through her daughter, Arlene, in Hospice. Both were from Belize in Central America. Bernarda had moved to the United States in 1981 and became a citizen in 1998. She was very proud to be a citizen of the United States of America.

Bernarda and Arlene became volunteers for Hospice and helped with Spanish speaking patients and families. Arlene went on to become a Registered Nurse and then joined our staff at Hospice.

If you needed any project completed all we had to do was ask these two ladies. They both had a knack for figuring out a simple solution. Everyone in our office loved Bernarda and her sweet smile and gentle spirit. She was happy to be a Hospice volunteer. It meant the world to her to be able to serve the Lord in this way. Humble is the word that described her, plus she had a very deep faith.

Gwen Louise Lloyd, the Bereavement Counselor for Hospice, shared with me how Bernarda helped her one day. She wrote these words and I quote:

"We all have God given gifts. One of mine is to give hope to others…to help others recognize their value…to inspire others. I do it in my personal life and I get paid to do it in the work force. But some days I need it. One day when I was feeling like I had the weight of the world on my shoulders and it was all slipping quickly, Bernarda stopped by my office, sat down and we talked. Her words were just what I needed to be reminded of and they sunk deeply in my heart. I knew she had gone through much in her life…far more than I. She said that it didn't matter what you went through in life, if you had Jesus…you had it all. In her simple, sincere way she summed up the true secret of life, peace and happiness. When you have Jesus, you have it all. Bernarda was a woman that had it all."

Gwen Louise continues:

"Bernarda was also a woman who believed that she could accomplish the impossible, hence she did. When I moved from the farm, I gave her my chickens. She and Arlene came out after a memorial service to get them. Bernarda was dressed in a pretty pink lace dress. The chickens escaped. I said well let's forget it for now…no way are we going to catch them. Bernarda, without a word, hiked up her dress, took off her shoes and started after them. As I watched, open mouthed, she caught them one by one. Not because she could run faster, but because she simply convinced the chickens that she could. Bernarda was a woman that did it, whatever the task, because it needed to be done."

Now she was facing a new task. As I stood beside her bed and looked into her eyes I asked her if she saw angels. She shook her head yes. Then I asked if she saw Jesus. Again, she shook her head yes.

She spoke words but her daughters and I could not understand them because of the oxygen mask over her face. Maybe we were not meant too. I asked her if I could pray and she shook her head yes again for the third time.

We prayed for the Lord's will, strength and courage to accept whatever that was, thanksgiving for all the blessings in Bernarda's life, and for a gentle crossing if the Lord was going to call her home on this day.

Bernarda had heard me speak of the stories of Death Can Be Beautiful. I told her a story one last time. She spoke again, but we could not understand her words.

Shortly after, Bernarda's breathing changed and she slipped into a coma. She looked comfortable and at peace. After a period of time she took three deep breaths and crossed into Heaven.

She looked so beautiful. Her complexion was smooth and she had a slight smile on her face. We knew her work on this earth was finished. Now she was in Heaven.

Her family came to say good-bye that evening in the Emergency Room after she had died. There were many tears. Bernarda had slipped away so fast and no one was prepared, except Bernarda.

She had been visiting her sister in Florida for a month and when she was leaving, told her sister, "This will be the last time we will see each other."

She made this statement two days before she died.

Arlene said they were driving Bernarda home from Florida and she looked back at her mother as she slept in the back seat and thought, *this is how Mom will look when she dies.*

Was the Lord preparing them both for what was about to happen?

As I walked around the funeral home the night of the visitation, I heard many people describing how Bernarda had touched their lives, how much she had meant to them, how they loved her. Nearly three hundred people signed the guest book that night and the day of the funeral.

The small church on the day of the funeral was filled to capacity with family and friends. Bernarda's favorite scriptures were read and favorite songs sung. The Pastor gave a wonderful sermon sharing thoughts about Bernarda and what she had taught him.

She once said to him, "Pastor, do I have to teach you everything?"

Not only was Bernarda humble, but she kept us humble as well.

At the close of the message, the Pastor said Bernarda had made a request for her funeral service. He asked the congregation to stand. Everyone was wondering what was coming next.

Then he said Bernarda wanted everyone to hug the people around them and say, "I love you."

How like her to plan the end of the service with a reminder of her love.

A short time after the funeral some friends took Bernarda's daughter, Arlene, fishing in honor of Bernarda's love of that sport. Arlene said she reeled in the biggest cat fish she had ever caught. She also brought home several other fish.

While sitting in the boat looking up at the sky and thinking of her mother, a beautiful butterfly came fluttering around the boat. It circled three times and then disappeared.

Arlene felt her mother's presence in that butterfly and she felt comfort. Several other times Arlene has had experiences of butterflies since her Mother died. God gave her these gifts of comfort.

After the death of a loved one it is a custom in Belize to light a candle for six months in mourning for that person. A short time before Bernarda died she told Arlene she only wanted her to light the candle for one month.

"One month is plenty of time to mourn for me," she said.

"Then it is time to get back to life."

Bernarda, thank you for touching our lives and letting us know you. Thank you for teaching us to love Jesus and each other. Thank you for teaching us how to live. We love you and we miss you.

A YOUNG MAN

He will gather the lambs with His arm, and carry them in His bosom, and gently lead those who are with young.
Isaiah 40:11

This story is difficult to write, but, it must be told. Today a Memorial Mass was held for a forty-three year old man with a lovely wife and three beautiful children, two girls fourteen and eleven, and a boy nine.

As I write this, my son is also forty-three years old with a lovely wife and three beautiful children. The short time I knew this family hit close to home.

This couple did a wonderful job preparing their children for what was to come, explaining illness, cancer, and the result of it all.

Their father had a brain tumor. Unfortunately, it was a tumor that caused pain. They all learned to cope the best they could and had love, help, and support from their families, friends, and church family.

When I visited the first time, the living room was the sick room. It was filled with the art of a loving young son who had drawn many pictures and cards for his Dad. The patient proudly pointed them out to me.

He and his wife told me something about each child. They shared how they met and their love of life. Each shared their faith and their love of God, even in this time of illness and death. There were tears but there was bravery as well.

The patient died on a Sunday. After the last Mass on that day, the priest came to be with the wife, children, parents, sibling, and friends.

It was the visitation for the patient because his wish was to be cremated. The two daughters wrote the most beautiful letters to their father. They brought tears to our eyes. The son drew another picture. Many life stories were told and more tears were shed.

The patient's mother said, "He lived a fuller life than most people do that live to an old age."

As I sat there, I tried to put myself in each person's shoes, especially the parent's shoes. It was difficult.

The Mass and the singing today at the funeral were beautiful. Part was in English and part in Spanish. The patient had met his wife in Costa Rica while in the U. S. Peace Corps, thus the English and Spanish at the Mass.

Siblings talked about their brother and friends spoke of him as well. They described him as intelligent, fun loving, analytical, and inquiring about life and spirituality. All said they would miss him.

His mother put everything together in these words: "He is not gone. He is right here in these three children and his wife. He will live on through them."

We do not understand why these things happen to young people with a spouse and a family and a bright future ahead of them. We can question.

I struggled with this death.

I asked myself, "How can you write about this in the book and say it is beautiful?"

God gave me the answer.

It was beautiful because three young children showed their love for their father through hugs, letters and art. It was real because siblings and friends struggled with anger and asking God why. It was beautiful because a mother was able to see her son live on through his wife and children. Could I have seen that?

Most of all it was beautiful and real because a young couple had faith and love of their Lord through this tragedy. They were weak at times but they were strong at other times too. They always had hoped there would be some miracle but the day he died there was peace on his face and in the home as well as tears.

They taught their children about death. They taught each other. Through it all, they loved each other and they loved God. They are an example to all of us.

THE BOOK OF LIFE

"Most assuredly, I say to you, whatever you ask the Father in My name He will give you."
John 16:23

When someone comes to Hospice a team is available to them. This team includes a nurse case manager, a social worker, a bath aide and a chaplain. The patient and family have the right to refuse the social worker and chaplain if they want. The patient I am writing about refused a chaplain. She was Catholic and did not see how a woman chaplain could be of any help.

As the few short weeks she had left on this earth passed, a close trusting relationship formed between her and her nurse. She began to ask spiritual and death and dying questions. The nurse gently asked if the chaplain could come and visit. After some thought, the patient reluctantly agreed.

I was greeted at the front door by one of the patient's six daughters; the patient also had two sons.
The first thing the daughter said was, "Please don't be insulted if my mother does not talk much. She is a very private person and has a hard time sharing her thoughts with people."
I assured her it would be alright, not to worry.

As I entered the room I could see the patient sizing me up. She asked her daughter to leave and close the door. Reluctantly, her daughter left the room. The patient asked me to sit down.
She took a deep breath and said, "OK, they said I needed to talk so here goes." Then she began to share her heart. I could see she had given this conversation much thought. She shared her fears of dying, her faith in God, some of her life stories, and family stories as well. Also, she shared a prayer book that

she had put together during her life. It had prayers for every occasion. We called it her Book of Life.

At one point her daughter knocked on the door, peaked in, and asked, "Is everything alright?"

"Yes" the patient replied, "Now close the door I'm not finished yet."

We talked for over two hours, each sharing with the other and speaking of issues that were bothering her. I shared stories of past patients as they were dying, some with the same concerns as hers.

At the end of this conversation she said, "I like you and I want you to come back again to talk."

We hugged and I left planning in my mind to come back the next week.

On my next visit two other daughters were present. They asked me to tell them the stories I had told their mother. I shared these plus more. They were some of the stories in this book.

During the visit I kept looking at the patient. She had declined since the last visit.

As I hugged her goodbye she whispered in my ear, "It won't be long but I'm ready."

Then she said louder so her daughters could hear, "Thank you for sharing the stories. They make me feel so much better."

As I left her home I thought about her complete faith and devotion to God and how privileged I was to have met her.

The next week I received a phone call from the office nurse. She reported the patient was rapidly declining and would I deliver some supplies to the home for the Hospice RN and family to use.

As I entered the patient's room I could see that she was in the dying process. She was not responding. I prayed with the family and gave them as much support and encouragement as I could.

Later that evening I received the call that she had died. I had the honor of staying with the family until the funeral home arrived. The Parish Priest also came.

We both visited with the family as they shared many memories of their mother. She had slipped away so quickly most of the family was not prepared, some were.

We sat at the bedside and leafed through her Book of Life. It is a precious memory for them to share with each other. As they read the prayers she picked out for each life situation they will remember their mother's faith in God and realize she is still teaching them how to live.

I TAKE IT BACK

"To him the doorkeeper opens, and the sheep hear his voice; and he calls his own sheep by name and leads them out."
John 10:3

During my years working at Hospice I had the pleasure of working with wonderful giving nurses. One of these nurses did not completely retire until she was eighty years old—and then she retired to get married. We all loved her.

The Hospice staff was in the habit of calling this nurse, Erna, and I, The Diamond Duo. Why? If there was a difficult patient they were assigned to us. Erna had a way of turning grouchy men into cooperative patients.

My job was to observe and back her up if needed. This story is an example.

One day Erna told me about a patient that was living in the nursing home. He had cancer and asked his son to put him in the nursing home to die. The patient had been in the military most of his life.

He stated, "I don't want to stick around and be miserable. I want it to be over."

This patient refused to get up to go to the bathroom and was refusing to go to the dining room to eat. He would not go out of his room for any social activities.

In addition, he stated proudly, "I do not believe in God and I certainly do not want a chaplain to visit me."

He had one mission to complete and that was to die.

Not bothered by his tirade, Erna told him to get up and get moving, especially to use the bathroom.

"You are perfectly capable to do this on your own," she told him.

Arrangements were made for him to go to the dining room to eat his meals. She would have none of his feeling sorry for himself and told him so. She said he needed to talk and a chaplain would be a good person to listen.

After much grumbling he finally agreed to let me come one time on two conditions. The first was Erna had to bring me to introduce us. The second was if I mentioned God one time, he would dismiss me quickly. I agreed to the challenge.

Underneath the rough and gruff exterior, this man was a delight. I'm not saying it was easy, no; it was touch and go at first. Eventually, we became comfortable when we visited. He loved telling stories about the wars he served in and the countries he visited. However, I always kept in mind not to mention God. I didn't want to be dismissed.

Erna worked wonders with this patient and soon he was eating in the dining room for meals and attending activities, especially those geared toward men's interests. The nursing home staff often commented about the change they saw in him. He was beginning to be happy to be alive.

Three months later, the patient brought up the forbidden subject, God. I quickly lowered my eyes afraid to react.

Finally he asked, "Aren't you going to say anything?"

"No," I replied, "You told me never to bring up God's name or you would dismiss me. I've grown quite fond of you and enjoy our visits, so I'm afraid to say anything."

"I take it back," he said as he looked directly into my eyes.

"I want to talk about God, and Heaven, and how to get there."

After that interchange we had many good discussions about the Lord. He was like a sponge wanting to soak up everything he could learn. He asked to be baptized and arrangements were made. Not only was he happy, he glowed. And his health became better.

It was decided the patient could go off Hospice and transfer to our step down program called Hand In Hand. He even was able to move to a senior apartment. His Hospice volunteer visited every week to play cards and check on him. If he started to decline he would come back to Hospice.

He was able to be on his own for a few months. During this time he enjoyed life and continued to learn about the Lord by reading the Bible.

When he became ill again he returned to the nursing home. Hospice was called in again.

"This will be it," he stated.

"But I promise not to cause so much trouble this time," he said as he smiled.

He asked Erna and me if we would be with him when he died. We said we would try our very best and if that was to happen the Lord would arrange it. He did.

We both stayed with him during the last hours before he died. Nursing home staff came one by one to say goodbye.

They kissed him on the forehead and hugged him. We spoke of how different he was from when he came to the nursing home the first time. Everyone was grieving the loss of someone they loved, not the angry man who was determined to die in a few days. I felt he could hear us speaking about him and I could picture him smiling.

God touches all of us during our lifetimes, even during the last months of our lives. It does not make a difference if we are twelve, forty, eighty, or a hundred. He loves us no matter what we have accomplished, or not accomplished, in this life. All He wants is for us to be with Him in eternity when He calls us home. It is our decision. This patient made that choice in the last months of his life.

MY BROTHER

"Not My will, but Yours be done."
Luke 22:42

This is a difficult story to write and I have been putting it off for months. During this time I have been asking myself, why am I not writing about my brother? Here is what I discovered.

When the first sibling in a family dies it is different than losing your parents. It brings to your mind, front and center, that you could be next. Dying had come to our generation. Yes, again, I have faced I am very human and at times my chaplain training goes out the window. My brother dying of cancer and a heart condition was close and personal.

Ernie and I have always called ourselves the "Seconds." He was the second born son and I was the second born daughter. But our similarities did not end there.

We both had had a desire to attend college. It was not possible for either of us to graduate for various reasons. We were the only two in our family who fought a weight problem. I confess I still fight that battle. We both had an interest in traveling and learning about new things.

I drew the line when he went bald. I was not about to follow suit on that one.

Fourteen years is the difference in our ages. Ernie did not get married until he was twenty-four years old. We were the only two living at home because all of our other siblings were married.

When I was in the eighth grade and a basketball cheerleader, he would drive the girls to the games. As I look back, I can see the patience he must have had with us as we giggled and talked about boys on our way home.

Life was good back then and very carefree.

After I married and moved out of the area, Ernie and his wife would come to visit. No matter how far away we were transferred, they would come. This helped my home sickness. We would have many good talks, sometimes long into the night.

I was living in Pennsylvania when I received a call from my brother telling me he had prostate cancer. Ernie had pulled a shoulder fixing his garage door and had rotator cuff surgery. Through complications during this time it was discovered he had cancer. What a blow. Not my brother.
This could not be happening, I thought.
Ernie did well with his first treatments and went into remission. We were all relieved.
After a period of time he called and said his PSA test was up again. This began round two. Ernie's cancer came and went over a period of eight years.

Toward the end of this time, his cancer spread to his brain.
He called me when he was in the hospital for tests and asked, "Am I dying?"
Sucking in my breath, I asked him, "Why do you think that?"
He said a priest came to visit him that day and before he entered the room read his chart hanging in a basket outside his room on the wall.
While reading the chart, the priest kept repeating out loud, "Oh no, oh no."
"What do you think that means?" he asked.
I told him, "I do not know why that would happen."
Down deep I knew what that meant. The news of his condition would not be good. I could not let myself think about it right then, let alone verbalize it.
Living in a different state from my brother, I found it hard to be both sister and chaplain from a distance.

The last time Ernie was in the hospital it was decided he should go onto Hospice. It was Friday and he was scheduled to go home in a few days.

Speaking to my sister-in-law on the phone that Friday evening, I had a difficult time settling down to sleep. I tossed and turned, finally getting up to lie on the sofa in our kitchen/family room. I did not want to keep my husband awake.
While lying on the sofa, I began to pray with my eyes closed. I was filled with emotions like many Hospice families.
Lord, I don't want him to die, but I don't want him to suffer either, I prayed.

Finally, crying, I was able to pray as Jesus prayed, not my will, Father, but your will be done.

Shortly after I finished praying, I heard a noise in the kitchen like a glass being set down on the counter. I had put the stove light on when I entered the room earlier.

Opening my eyes, I looked around the room and said, "Jay, is that you?"

I thought my husband had gotten up to check on me. I did not see anyone.

Settling down again on the sofa, I began to pray a second time. A peace began to cover me like a blanket. Suddenly I heard the noise again, only louder.

Continuing to feel the peace and beginning to feel a presence I asked, "Ernie, is that you? And Mom, you are here with him too aren't you? I love you both."

I cried softly, feeling their love.

Then I prayed, thank you Lord, for this gift.

I felt awed and grateful by the gift of being able to say good-bye.

Shortly after this happened I was able to go back to bed and fall asleep.

The next morning I received a phone call from my nephew telling me my brother had died. Ernie did not make it home. God called him to Heaven, to His home.

My husband and I packed our clothes and started the journey to Illinois for the funeral. Many things went through my mind and I did not always feel the peace I felt the night before, but, I continued to feel thankful for the gift of presence and the gift of being able to say good-bye that I had received from the Lord.

I couldn't wait to see my family and share my story with my oldest brother, who we were staying with.

When we arrived, I felt excitement as I hurried into his home. We both cried and hugged.

Then I said, "I have something to tell you that happened Friday night."

"And I have something to tell you," he replied.

Being the gentleman he is, he let me speak first. I talked as fast as I could with my brother smiling as I told my story.

When I had run out of breath he asked, "What time did this happen?"

I told him the time.

He grinned and said, "They stopped by to see me first about thirty minutes before you said they were at your house and they awoke me out of a sound sleep."

As we discussed the stories again, we decided it must take people in Heaven thirty minutes to travel from Illinois to Missouri, that is, unless they stopped to visit other people along the way.

In no way do I mean to make light of my brother dying, it hurt very much, but sharing the story of the visits from Ernie and Mom the night he died helped our family through the days of the funeral and beyond. We knew without a doubt where Ernie was—with the Lord. Neither my oldest brother nor I could see Ernie or our mother, but both of us could feel their presence and their love and knew they were there.

This experience happened several years ago. We both remember it vividly and continue to thank God for the memory and the gift.

A blessing that comes with funerals and large families is, people come from far and near. Being together and reminiscing about old times helps lesson the grief a little. After the funeral we gathered at a large restaurant and did just that. I know Ernie would have loved seeing us all together. We did it in his honor.

BERTHA

"She speaks with wisdom, and faithful instruction is on her tongue"
Proverbs 31:26

Sometimes God sends wonderful people into our lives that we meet at a later time again. That is exactly what happened when I met Bertha's daughter, Barbara.

The first time I met Barbara was when I became a chaplain and we worked together at the same hospital. Then we lost contact when I moved to marry my husband in another state. Hospice brought us back together again.

When my friend's mother came on Hospice we were happy to see each other again. We caught up on the years that had past and then she took me in to meet her mother.

Her mother was a warm, smiling lady who was comfortable with her illness and glowed as she told me how she was looking forward to meeting the Lord and her family that had gone on before her. What a delightful lady.

Have you ever met someone who was ill and they immediately made you feel comfortable? Someone who is bed bound, but is interested in what is happening in the outside world and wants you to tell them all about it? This describes Barbara's mother. Add to that, she also enjoyed sharing her love of the Lord with everyone.

From time to time, Bertha would write stories and prayers that came to her mind. Following is a beautiful prayer she wrote while on a drive with her husband. She rewrote it into a prayer-song in 1983 and Barbara set it to music for her.

Good morning, God!
The sky's so blue
The air's so clear

Heaven's glory's shining through.

God morning, God!
Go with me today.
Guide my thoughts, my words,
My feet along the way.

Give me a task that only I can do.
Let me be brave and strong
And to Thy way be true.
Good morning, God!

What wonderful treasures she left for her family to hold dear and close to their hearts.

Following is an excerpt from Bertha's ninetieth birthday party written by her daughter Barbara:

"Bertha was raised in a Christian home and gave her heart to Jesus when she was nine years old. Here is the story of her conversion in her own words: 'As the oldest child I resented some of the responsibilities I had to assume. At times I was extremely stubborn, adamantly refusing to be obedient. Being a regular attendant at church, I knew that someday I would have to make a decision about yielding my life to Christ. I felt guilt about my stubbornness and just couldn't sleep as I should. One night I just got out of bed, knelt and gave my life to God, promising to follow in all ways, but especially asking help to overcome my problems. Then I made a public profession at our next revival, and was baptized in a creek when the weather got warmer. Being a Christian means letting Jesus be Lord of my life. It means striving to be Christ-like in all things. It means being able to walk daily in direct communication with God. It means being able to let others see Jesus in me.'"

Meeting Bertha in her last weeks of her life, I can tell you she did exactly that—let others see Jesus in her. She was an example to all of her family especially during the illness and death of her husband. Barbara wrote about it and I quote her again:

"Bertha was a wonderful nurse and companion and saw him through, holding his hand or stroking his brow through the long vigil. Her serenity and calm ministered to her entire family. When he drew his last breath, she felt his spirit soar away. Bertha's children, standing beside her, witnessed a peaceful countenance and a beautiful smile on her face as she clasped her hands together in silent prayer and released her lifelong companion into the arms of Jesus. They had been married fifty three years. As Bertha's children and grandchildren walked with her through the final days of Ed's earthly life, she taught them how to deal with the reality of death in a very natural way and never let them forget that this was not the end, it was the beginning of eternal life. She focused on comforting them and not on her own needs, as was, and still is, the pattern of her life—always putting others first."

Now it was Bertha's turn to make the journey from this earth to Heaven. It was time for her family to practice everything she taught them and they did it well.

Many were present as she passed through her last hours. They took turns beside the bed, saying their good-byes. Bertha was very peaceful and she crossed to the other side very gently.

Her granddaughters helped the Hospice nurse prepare their grandmother's body before the funeral home arrived. It was a beautiful last gift for them to give her.

Bertha died when she was ninety-one years old. She lived a long life serving the Lord, loving her family, and teaching them the many lessons of how to live and then how to die.

VON

Love the Lord your God with all your heart and with all your soul and with all your mind. This is the first and greatest commandment. And the second is like it: Love your neighbor as yourself.
  Matthew 22:37

This story is about Von, my friend Barbara's husband.

Von's health was declining during his mother-in-law's illness and journey to Heaven. We became acquainted during that time.

Von had a deep spirituality which he and Barbara shared in the songs they wrote and recorded. He led a full life, using the talents and gifts God gave him, loving God and his neighbor.

He not only was a musician, but also an artist, photographer, and woodcarver. With his father, he was a rancher raising alfalfa, cotton and raisin grapes. They also had hundreds of bee hives. Later in life he managed two camps, touching the lives of many people while he worked there with his beloved wife at his side.

One of the songs Von and Barbara wrote was Jesus Will Lead the Way Through. The first verse and chorus especially touched me. I think it will comfort you as well. It goes like this:

In this world of sorrows, doubts and miseries, I have
found the answer, I have found the key. Even though I
cannot see what lies ahead I know the Lord is there beside
me. So I've nothing more to dread.

Jesus will lead the way through. Oh, Jesus will lead
the way through. Though the dark sea may surround me;

Jesus will lead the way through.

I believe these words written years before helped Von, Barbara, and all of the family cope. I know they have helped me.

During his last days, he was surrounded by family, friends, and love. On one of my last visits I asked Von if he had seen Jesus.

"No," he replied, "But I've seen Barbara with a man standing behind her. What could that mean?"

I assured him, "That is Barbara's angel. God has sent him to protect and guide her after you are gone. It is a gift from the Lord that you were able to see him."

He was comforted by this. They had had a good marriage and enjoyed serving the Lord together but he needed God's promise that she would be taken care of.

He did not want to leave, but knew it was God's time. He began to prepare himself and his family. It was beautiful to observe.

A few days before Von died, Barbara gave me a series of three children's books by Joel Anderson. They were about Faith, Love, and Eternity. She said she thought I could use them in my ministry. I looked through the books. They were excellent and I knew I would be able to read them to children and grandchildren of dying patients. However, I did not know how soon that would be.

On the Sunday before Von died multiple family and friends visited, many of them children. As I watched everyone come and go out of Von's room I felt the Lord telling me to read the book, Tell Me About Eternity, to the children. I mentioned this to Barbara. She gathered all of them into the living room and I began to read and show the beautiful pictures in the book.

These children were different ages but they all listened intently. I watched each face as they soaked in the information about birth and death. After the story ended they shared questions and comments. One comment I remember was from a granddaughter.

She said, "We have to wait our turn to see Papa in Heaven."

I looked puzzled at the moms and grandmothers listening. They said to ask Barbara.

Barbara told me two stories that happened with the children and their Papa over the weekend. The first one was two of the granddaughters were visiting. They asked to see Papa and pray with him.

After their prayer, one of them asked, "Papa, can we go to Heaven with you?"

Papa, smiling, said, "No, I wish you could, but you have to wait until the Lord tells you it is time for you to go."

The girls were satisfied with his answer. They kissed him and went on to play. This story explained the comment from the granddaughter after I read, Tell Me About Eternity.

The second story happened on Sunday, the day before Von died. That time all of the grandchildren who were present gathered in Papa's room and stood around the bed. They sang and sang. Von was not responding much by that time, but I know he could hear his little angels' voices. The last song they sang for Papa was, Jesus Loves Me.

Can you picture that beautiful scene? I can.

Von had a peaceful crossing into Heaven the next day. His family and friends took turns sitting beside the bed through those last hours, speaking messages of love and other things they needed to say to him.

Two hours before he died, I asked Barbara if she had given Von permission to cross over to be with the Lord. She immediately went to his bedside and gave him permission. He puckered his lips for one last kiss.

Von and Barbara had a daughter who died at the age of sixteen from cancer. When she died, Von put his hands under her body, lifting her. He thanked the Lord for the gift of a daughter and then gave her back to Him.

As Von was taking his last breaths, Barbara and all of the children did the same. They put their hands under him and thanked God for the gift of husband, father, grandfather, and friend. Then they gave him back to the Lord.

Music was playing softly during this time, songs Von had written and favorites he enjoyed listening to. When his last moments came, his daughter-in-law turned up the volume. The song playing was, Beyond The Sounds Of Battle There's Victory For Me.

As I mentioned earlier, Von was an artist and woodcarver. He took many pieces of wood and transformed them into something beautiful.

In the woods on one of the camps he managed, he saw a fallen tree after a storm. He took it back to his workshop, cut it, planed it and then set it aside planning to use it someday for what he did not know.

When he died it was still unused, but not for long. Family and friends lovingly took this wood and made his casket, his final resting place. There was just enough wood. After placing him in the casket, they placed a quilt around his body made by his mother.

Von's visitation and funeral were beautiful. His life was displayed by pictures and things he loved, as well as his music in CD's and sheet music. Mementos were given to those who came. One of his sons, a minister, preached his funeral. Many attended.

There was a sign hanging above Von's hospital bed that read, "Love transcends all time….it's a voice in the heart that never stops singing." These are the words engraved on one side of his tombstone along with a picture of Von and Barbara facing each other, smiling.

His tombstone is unusual. It is a black stone bench that faces the Eastern sky. The family wanted it to be a place of comfort and rest to everyone. On the other side of the bench this scripture from Isaiah 32:18 is engraved, "My people will dwell in a peaceful habitation, in secure dwellings, and in quiet resting places."

Barbara and the family miss Von very much, but they have his legacy of music, his wood carvings, and the lessons he taught them on how to love God and their neighbor to comfort them. Like the title of the song, Jesus will lead the way through.

A LESSON LEARNED

Show me Your ways, O Lord; teach me Your paths. Lead me in Your truth and teach me, for You are the God of my salvation; On You I wait all the day.
   Psalm 25:4-5

This story is not about death. It is a story about a lesson God taught me about living. A lesson I needed to learn to be a better chaplain. Several years ago, on a beautiful Fall Sunday afternoon in October, my husband had a heart attack. Thank God he survived.

The day before was Jay's fifty-fifth birthday. Several couples we were friends with had gotten together to go out to dinner for this occasion. Then we gathered at one of their homes to have birthday cake and coffee.

The men sat around the table talking and kidding each other as the women prepared to serve the dessert.

One of the men said, "Jay, you know what happens when you turn fifty-five don't you?"

"No," Jay replied, "What happens?"

"You have a heart attack," he said.

Everyone laughed and went on to enjoy the evening.

The next morning after church, we went to breakfast with another couple. We again were celebrating Jay's birthday. I remember he ordered stuffed French toast with bananas and walnuts. Isn't it strange how some things are imbedded in our memory?

After breakfast Jay and I decided to attend the antique show at the Fair Grounds before putting on a program at a local nursing home.

We had been at the show for only a few minutes when Jay said, "I don't feel well. Come with me."

I followed him as we made our way to the restroom and then waited outside the door. He did not come out for what seemed like a long time. As I waited, I thought of what he had ordered for breakfast.

Did this make him sick? I thought.

By this time I began to panic and stopped a man walking by and asked him to check on my sick husband in the restroom. Just then Jay walked out, stumbling and very gray in color.

"I think I'm having a heart attack," he said.

Things began to move fast. We laid Jay on the floor and a crowd began to gather. An antique dealer came over and told us she was a retired cardiac nurse and could she help. Another woman said she worked in the Emergency Room at one of our hospitals and she could help. Someone offered to call 911.

I remember thinking at the time; *God is taking care of us, sending us the right people to help.*

The Fire Department arrived, then the ambulance.

As Jay lay on the floor, my hospital experience flashed through my mind.

He is in big trouble, I thought.

God, please help him, I prayed.

I arrived at the hospital first because the ambulance staff continued to work on Jay a long time in the ambulance parked outside the Fair Grounds building. The ER nurse suggested I go ahead and wait for Jay at the hospital. As I drove, many thoughts and prayers went through my mind.

My main thought was, *Is Jay dying, Lord? Please help him.*

One of the chaplains was standing at the ER door when I walked in. We had worked together several years in the hospital before I worked for Hospice. She asked me who I was visiting.

"They are bringing Jay in," I replied, "He is having a heart attack."

She said as she hugged me, "Oh Ellen, you are the case I am waiting for. I did not connect the name when they gave it to me."

The ambulance arrived shortly after. Things began to move fast. The cardiologist was waiting to do an angiogram, along with the heart team in case they were needed.

The chaplain helped me make phone calls and friends began to arrive. I was feeling numb at this point.

Jay's main artery was 100% blocked. It was called the "widow maker," the doctor said, but thank God a stent took care of it. They had been prepared to do open heart surgery if it was needed.

Then the doctor said, "Tell your husband not to quit his day job. He tried to be a comedian in there telling us jokes."

Everyone laughed. It was the relief we needed after the intense time of waiting. It made us feel Jay would be all right.

To this day, Jay does not remember the jokes he told before the procedure started.

All he can remember is the anesthesiologist chuckling several times and the doctor saying, "We have work to do here."

Then he was put out.

Jay was put in Intensive Care overnight and I stayed in a waiting room close by. A wonderful neighbor stayed with me. It was comforting to have her support and the support of our family and friends during this time.

I visited Jay when family was allowed to come into Intensive Care.

At one of these visits he said, "I have something to tell you. When I was lying in the ambulance at the Fair Grounds I heard a voice. It was not the ambulance staff, this voice came from the window side of the ambulance. It said, 'Jay, you are going to be all right.'"

He continued, "I felt so peaceful, Ellen. I think it was the Lord."

We smiled as we looked at each other with tears in our eyes.

Jay was awake and restless in the middle of the night. The staff let me come in and sit with him.

In those days you had to lie flat on your back for several hours after an angiogram and stint. He was uncomfortable and had back pain. Then things changed on the monitor and the staff asked me to step out.

Something was wrong. I was scared. I kept thinking how during Jay's heart attack I had lost all chaplain skills and had become all wife. I wasn't sure how I felt about it.

Again, I wondered, *is Jay going to die?*

After what seemed like an eternity, the nurse called me back into Intensive Care. Jay was awake but I could tell He was exhausted by the happenings of the day and he was pale again. The nurse explained he had had a bad spell but was doing better now and I could stay for a few minutes.

When she left, Jay took my hand.

He had a peaceful look on his face as he said, "Ellen, the next time the Lord comes to get me can I go?"

All of my breath left me.

My mind raced as I gripped the rail of the bed and I said a very selfish thing, "But what about me?"

Then very clearly I heard the Lord's voice say to me in my mind, "Ellen, what about all the times you stood by a patient's bedside and helped families tell their loved ones it was all right to go to Heaven and be with Me? Now it is time to tell Jay."

I remembered earlier when Jay was laying on the floor at the Fair Grounds I repeated many times, "Hold on, Honey. Don't' leave me."

Now God was asking me to do the unthinkable. I felt firsthand what those families had felt. What a lesson God was teaching me.

Screaming inside, with tears flowing down my face, I said, "Yes, Jay, the next time the Lord comes to get you, you can go."

Jay is still with me today and I am very thankful. The Lord asked for my obedience. The valuable lesson I learned that day has helped me in my ministry through the years. When I stand at the bedside of a dying patient with their family, I hope I am a gentler chaplain, sharing their feelings as they give permission to their loved one to cross over to the other side.

TAKE JESUS' HAND

Even there Your hand shall lead me, and Your right hand shall hold me.
Psalm 139:10

One bright sunshiny late afternoon I was leaving the patient's home who wanted to take me with him to Heaven. I felt the Lord's gentle nudge to visit another patient that lived in a town a few miles away. Due to the lateness of the hour, I did not want to drive all the way back to Springfield, and then to the town where this patient lived.

Go back into the house and ask directions on how to drive across country, I thought. There were three men in the home at the time. All three gave me different directions.

It went something like this, "Go to the Jones farm then turn left until you come to the Smith place and turn south."

"No, she needs to go to the four corners by the…etc."

Well, you get the idea. I went back to the car, sat there for a few minutes and prayed, Lord, I need your help. I know you want me to go visit this patient. Please let me take all of these directions and find the town.

I started out looking for landmarks, mailboxes, and trees that had broken down in recent storms. Finally I spotted a welcome sight in the distance—the town's water tower.

As I drove into the driveway of my patient's home I saw our Social Worker's car parked close. Lord, help me to know why you wanted me to come, I prayed. I soon found out.

Just as I walked up onto the porch and put my hand up to knock, the Social Worker opened the door and said, "I knew you were coming."

"How did you know?" I asked.

"When I was leaving another patient's home the Lord nudged me to come here."

"Well, about forty five minutes ago this patient said to me, 'Sure wish that chaplain would come. I have something to tell her.' Knowing that direct line you have sometimes, I thought you would be coming soon."

The Social Worker left shortly after, giving the patient an opportunity to talk.

This patient had shared many personal and private thoughts in our visits. He told me many times he knew God had forgiven him for the things he had done in his lifetime, but was having a hard time forgiving himself. He shared with me other concerns. I tried to reassure him Jesus died for all of our sins not just a few of them.

Several times he told me about a dream that kept reoccurring. He said he could see himself in a line waiting to get to Heaven.

"Many people are in front of me so it will be awhile."

Then he would say the next time, "There's still people in front of me, but I'm getting closer."

The last visit we had he said, "There's only a few people in front of me. It won't be long now."

Today he had something else to share with me.

"I have something to tell you," he began.

"This morning I had a vision. It was not a dream. I was not asleep. You, my wife, and I were walking together up a path. We came to a gate and stopped there to look through. There we saw Jesus standing on a small hill. Jesus began walking down the hill and came toward us. Then He opened the gate and held out His hand. I took His hand and you and my wife stayed on the other side."

He continued, "The path was very narrow and only one person could walk on it at a time. Jesus went first and I followed. Then Jesus reached for a broom that was leaning on the fence beside the gate and He began to sweep the path. As He swept the path it became wider and wider like a California freeway. It became as white as snow."

The patient used his hands as he related his vision to me. Especially, when he told of Jesus opening the gate and then when he told of the California Freeway he held out his hands and arms as wide as he could. He painted a vivid picture.

Then the patient leaned back in his chair, crossed his arms, and just looked at me. Lord, he wants me to interpret his vision. Please give me the words to say, I prayed.

I remembered our discussions in prior visits and then these words came to me, "Jesus is showing you He has forgiven all of your sins in this vision and He has swept them clean. You are now as white as snow."

"You got it! You got it!" he said.

"Seeing this has made me feel better. I am now ready to go. I can forgive myself."

The patient's wife came home from grocery shopping and I prepared to leave. I only told her we had a good visit because I wanted him to share his story with her if he chose.

The day the patient related his story to me was a Thursday. The next day, Friday, he began to decline rapidly. Hospice delivered a bed and other equipment needed to help make him comfortable. His stepchildren also came to give their support.

On Sunday morning about 4:00A.M., I received a phone call from the patient's wife.

She said, "He has been in a coma since midnight, Friday night. Things are beginning to change and I think it is close. Can you come?"

I got there as fast as I could.

As I entered the living room I could see many people surrounding the bed. The patient's minister was there. We knew each other from before, working with other families. He was pastor of a small church and said he needed to go home and get ready to teach Sunday school and have church.

The children had been present since Friday night and they asked if it would be alright if they went home to shower and get some rest. The patient's wife and I settled in for our watch.

As we sat beside the bed we quietly talked about their life together and how the patient always said she was his Angel because she took such good care of him.

She said, "I will miss him so."

The patient loved to be read to so I read his favorite devotionals and his favorite scriptures.

During a quiet time I heard the Lord say to me in my mind, "The scene is set."

I thought about this. Then I remembered the vision the patient told me about on Thursday.

The patient was lying in bed with his wife sitting on one side and me on the other, both of us holding his hands. Yes, the scene was set.

I asked the wife if her husband had told her about his vision. She said no. I shared with her how the vision began, with her, her husband, and I walking up a path together.

I then began to repeat the vision to the patient.

"We are walking up the path together," I said, "and we are coming to a gate. We are looking through the gate. Can you see Jesus standing on the hill?"

The patient squeezed our hands and smiled. His wife grasped. He had not moved or responded since Friday night. This was a gift and a blessing.

I continued, "Jesus is walking up to the gate. Now He is opening the gate and holding out His hand. Take His hand. Everything will be alright. Your wife will be alright, her children will take good care of her. All of your family will be alright too. Take Jesus' hand and walk into Heaven."

During a period of about five minutes the patient took a few more breaths and peacefully died. What a beautiful death.

Can you see how much God loves us? He knows us so well and blesses us with exactly what we need to feel His comfort and peace as we cross over to the other side to be with Him. The vision showed this man God's love and forgiveness. His dreams of standing in line also showed him some concept of the timing of his death.

The patient's funeral was a large one. He was a politician in his town and many people knew him. I arrived early but the parking lot was already filled.

I had made arrangements to come early because my husband was singing at the funeral. The patient had requested this. I had given him my husband's tape months before and he listened to it often. He had picked the songs he wanted Jay to sing for his funeral.

As I entered the funeral home, the director met me at the door. He asked me to follow him. I told him I was meeting Jay but he said no I needed to come with him. He could sense I was puzzled.

Then he said, "No one told you did they?"

"Told me what?" I asked.

He replied, "Apparently the patient told you about some vision he had. His wife wants you to tell about it at the funeral. I take it no one called to tell you."

My knees went weak. I was not prepared. The funeral director took me into the minister's room where three men sat. They were all taking part in the service.

When I sat down they said, "We are making you go last because you have this special story to tell."

Was I nervous? Yes. Not only was I to speak, I had to be last.

Then I thought, *look on the bright side. Now you have time to prepare.*

As we entered the parlor where the service was to be held, there was standing room only. My husband gave me a smile and I began to feel calmer. I gave him a look of thanks for his support.

In the front row were the patient's wife, her children, and the patient's children from out of state. I knew then that I was there to tell the story of the vision to them.

The patient's children were part of his story of regret and need for forgiveness. They needed to know how God had forgiven their father and that God wanted them to forgive him as well.

The majority of the time I spoke, I looked directly at them. After the service they came up immediately.

We hugged and they said "Thank you."

That was all that was needed, a simple thank you and a hug. God had done His work. The family could begin the forgiving process and perhaps then feel peace.

THE MESSAGE

"I will never leave you nor forsake you."
Hebrews 13:5

Now I would like to tell you the message Jesus gave my Angel Man years ago. He said, "Jesus said for us not to be afraid to die."

He continued, "God the Father would always, always send someone from the other side to be with us and walk us across."

"One of three things will happen," Jesus told the Angel Man.

"The first," the Angel Man said, "is someone may come to walk you across that you know, like a spouse who has gone before, or a parent, grandparent, child, or friend. The second thing, God may choose to send an angel or a room full of angels to walk you across. And the third thing is, sometimes Jesus himself will come." Jesus repeated several times for us not to be afraid.

What a wonderful gift God has given us through this Angel Man's message. He shared the message with me and said Jesus told him to tell me to pass it on to you. I have tried to do this in these stories I have written. God is always with us when we are dying and in addition He sends someone to be there for us as we cross over to the other side.

I have often thought, *what a privilege it would be to be the designated person God has assigned to walk someone to the other side and take them to meet Him for the first time.*

What a mission. What a comfort it is to realize that our loved ones did not die alone, even if we were not there with them.

So often people have come up after a speaking engagement and said to me, "I feel so much better."

They share with me how they had just left the room for a few minutes and their loved one died during that time or how they fell asleep or went home from the hospital to take a shower and it happened without their being there.

You can always rest assured they did not die alone. God sent just the right person, angel, or Jesus to walk them across.

I firmly believe that God plans who will be present with us on this earth when we die. So many times the Hospice staff has witnessed this. Sometimes the patient waits until a certain family member or friend arrives.

Always remember, the patient can hear you speak until the very end. If they hear you say someone is coming at a certain time they will wait until that person arrives, if that is the way it is supposed to be according to God's will. This will happen even though they cannot respond.

Always tell them how much you love them, tell them you are there with them, and for them to feel God's peace as they walk across to be with those who have gone before.

Sometimes patients wait to die until someone leaves the room or they die before someone arrives. This appears to happen because they feel it will hurt that person too much to see them take their last breath.

If you remember, this is what happened when my mother died. Yes, I felt hurt at first, but later I understood why it happened.

God has allowed me to go through many personal experiences in my life and later I used those experiences to understand, in some way, what the other person is going through. I thank Him for each and every one and am grateful when I can use them to help others.

THE FIRST DAY OF THE WEEK

Finally, Brethren, farewell. Become complete. Be of good comfort, be of one mind, live in peace: and the God of love and peace will be with you.
2 Corinthians 13:11

As I have been writing these stories, I wondered and prayed about how I should write the last chapter. One Easter Sunday I received my answer.

Bishop Liebreck had 7:00 o'clock Mass that morning. He took his message from 2 Corinthians 13:11. This scripture relates exactly what I would like you to remember.

As God made each of us unique and special, so too are our deaths unique and special. Picture the Gentle Shepherd waiting for us on the other side with his arms stretched out welcoming us. Thinking about our own death or the death of our loved ones is scary and devastating, but when you picture the Lord waiting, a peace will come over you.

Close your eyes and picture it……..feel it. Imagine the love God the Father has for you. He sent His Son to spend time with us and to teach us. Then Jesus died for us and that is love in the purest form.

We can always go to the Father with our feelings and doubts. Jesus did. He prayed to the Father many times in the Bible. You can go to the Father with your fears of your own death or that of a loved one. He understands. He lost His Son.

If you are facing the loss of a loved one and caring for them, take your burden to the Father. I promise He will help you. All you have to do is ask and then accept the help. God is a wonderful caregiver.

If you are facing a terminal illness yourself, give it to the Lord. Close your eyes and picture being held in the Father's arms. Feel His love and comfort. Tell Him what you are feeling. He will understand. He will wait during your tears and regrets. We all have them. Then feel the peace. Let Him calm the waves. When it is time for you to cross over to Heaven He will be there waiting along with the other loved ones who have gone before you. It will be the first day of the week—your first day in Heaven. You will be complete. You will be home.

References:

The New King James
New International Version
New American Bible